Water Snake

Water Snake Pet Owner's Guide

Water Snakes Care, Behavior, Diet, Interacting, Costs and Health.

By

Ben Team

Table of Contents

About the Author

The author, Ben Team, is an environmental educator and author with nearly 20 years of professional reptile-keeping experience.

Ben currently maintains www.FootstepsInTheForest.com, where he shares information, narration and observations of the natural world.

Foreword

North American water snakes are some of the most interesting reptiles in all of the New World. Unlike most other snakes, who are primarily terrestrial animals, water snakes live an amphibious existence. They split their time between land and fresh water, although they also venture into the trees overhanging rivers and lakes.

Unlike a lot of other snakes, who exhibit well-defined, rigid behaviors and life strategies, water snakes are often very flexible. Many are capable of adapting to changing environmental conditions and prey populations, and several routinely show up in man-made reservoirs, including backyard ponds.

While a few of the recognized species and subspecies are experiencing population declines, others are as abundant as they ever were – reinforcing the idea that these are highly adaptable serpents.

Given this adaptability, it is not surprising that most water snake species adapt well to captivity. Most eat readily and experience relatively few health problems, when provided with appropriate husbandry. Some even become relatively tame over time.

But to have a good chance at successful maintenance, you'll have to learn about water snakes (especially the species you elect to keep), their habitats and the ways in which other keepers maintain them.

And you can begin this journey on the following pages.

PART I: WATER SNAKES

Properly caring for any animal requires an understanding of the species and its place in the natural world. This includes digesting subjects as disparate as anatomy and ecology, diet and geography, and reproduction and physiology.

It is only by learning what your pet is, how it lives, what it does that you can achieve the primary goal of animal husbandry: Providing your pet with the highest quality of life possible.

Chapter 1: Physical Description and Anatomy

Although every water snake (*Nerodia* spp.) species has unique characteristics and features that distinguish them from other water snakes, they all share a few similarities. For example, most are thick-bodied, they all have keeled scales and most have relatively large heads for their body size.

Size

Water snakes are medium-sized snakes that range from about 24 to 60 inches in length (60 to 152 centimeters). Females reach larger sizes than the males do, but there is some overlap. Newborn water snakes are usually between 8 and 12 inches in length (20 to 30 centimeters).

Generally speaking, the water snakes living in the southern portions of the United States reach larger sizes than their counterparts living in the north. However, there are also size differences between the various species and subspecies too. Brown (*Nerodia taxispilota*), green (*Nerodia cyclopion*) and northern water snakes (*Nerodia sipedon*) are typically the largest species, while banded (*Nerodia fasciata*), plainbelly (*Nerodia erythrogaster*) and diamondback (*Nerodia rhombifer*) are usually somewhat smaller.

Scalation

Water snakes are clad in keeled, rather than smooth, scales along their backs and sides. This gives them a slightly rougher feel than kingsnakes and pythons.

They have large, plate-like ventral scales, which help them to crawl across the ground. They possess a divided, rather than single, anal plate, which is a criterion used to distinguish them from the cottonmouth (*Agkistrodon piscivorous*), with whom they are often confused.

Their heads are clad in a combination of large plate-like scales, and smaller, granular scales. The exact pattern and layout of these scales varies from one species to the next.

Color and Pattern

Water snakes exhibit a great deal of color and pattern variation. Not only do the different species possess different colors and patterns, but there is a great deal of variation between members of the same species or subspecies. Additionally, several species of water snakes undergo an ontogenetic (age-related) shift in color and pattern.

The color patterns of the most commonly kept water snakes are described below:

Northern Water Snake

Northern water snakes are generally clade in light tan and dark brown tones, although those living in the southern end of their range -- particularly the midland water snake (*Nerodia sipedon pleuralis*) – also display red and orange tones as well. Northern water snakes generally give the impression of a banded snake, although some individuals are better described as featuring blotches.

Banded Water Snake

Banded water snakes exhibit an excellent example of convergent evolution, as they strongly resemble the southernmost-dwelling northern water snakes, who they replace with decreasing latitude. As their name implies, they generally feature a banded pattern, which may feature colors ranging from dark brown to straw to red. The western subspecies – the broad-banded water snake (*Nerodia fasciata confluens*) – exhibits very wide, irregularly shaped bands, which are generally separated by light-colored borders.

Diamondback Water Snake

Diamondback water snakes are usually some combination of green and brown or olive colors. As their name implies, their reticulated pattern creates a series of vaguely diamond-shaped markings down the center of the back.

Plainbelly Water Snake

Although they exhibit a pattern reminiscent of northern water snakes at birth, plainbelly water snakes undergo a distinct ontogenetic color change as they mature. By the time they are adults, most have dark, unmarked dorsal surfaces and solid-colored ventral surfaces. The color of the ventral surface ranges from red to yellow, and differs from one subspecies to the next.

Brown Water Snake

As their name suggests, brown water snakes are clad in various brown tones. Usually, their ground color is a lighter shade of brown, while the square or rectangular blotches that cover their back and sides are a darker shade of brown. As they age, many brown water snakes become darker.

Green Water Snake

Green and Florida water snakes (some authorities consider them different species) are both generally olive to green snakes. They typically feature bold, dark markings as juveniles, but these tend to fade as the snakes mature.

Eyes and Ears

Water snakes see movement well, but their visual acuity is limited. However, their limited vision works well in both light and dark conditions.

While vision is not the most important sensory pathway for water snakes, it does play an important role in the lives of water snakes and provides them with a number of advantages.

Snakes lack moveable eyelids, meaning that their eyes are open at all times – even while they sleep. In fact, it can be difficult (or impossible) to tell whether a motionless snake is sleeping or awake. To protect their eyes, snakes have a clear scale covering each eye, called the spectacle. Like all other scales on the snake's body, they shed their spectacles periodically.

Water snakes have variably colored irises and round. While round pupils are frequently presumed to be a trait associated with diurnal activity patterns, research indicates that such eyes are more likely an adaptation to prowling – rather than ambush-oriented – hunting styles. (F. BRISCHOUX, 2010)

Like all other snakes, water snakes lack external ears entirely and only possess rudimentary inner ears. Although scientists debate the precise extent to which snakes can hear airborne sounds (if at all), it is clear that they do not hear airborne sounds well.

Nevertheless, snakes readily detect vibrations through direct contact with the substrate, which allows them to detect the footsteps of approaching predators.

The Tongue, Nose and Vomeronasal Organ

The forked tongue of snakes is one of their most famous characteristics. The tongue is solely a sensory organ that plays no role in feeding or sound production.

The tongue extends from the mouth to collect volatile particles from the environment. Then, when the tongue is withdrawn, it transfers these particles to the vomeronasal organ. The vomeronasal organ provides the snakes with an additional chemical sense, somewhat akin to smell or taste.

The vomeronasal organ (located in the roof of the mouth), has two openings – one for each tip of the snake's tongue. This allows snakes to process directional information picked up by the tongue. Snakes also use their nostrils to detect airborne chemicals in the environment, and have a very strong sense of smell.

Mouth and Teeth

Water snakes have a mouth full of sharp, recurved teeth, primarily designed for catching and holding prey.

The teeth are attached rather weekly to the surface of the jawbones. Like all other snakes, water snakes continually lose and replace teeth throughout their lives. Sometimes keepers will find shed teeth in their snake's cage or emerging from feces.

When at rest, many of the teeth are covered by gum tissue; when the snake's teeth penetrate the skin of their prey, the gums are pushed down, exposing the teeth.

Vent

Water snakes have a small opening – called the vent – on their ventral surface, near the base of the tail. The vent leads directly to the cloaca, and serves as the final exit point for waste, urates and their offspring.

When snakes defecate, release urates or copulate, the vent opens slightly.

Tail

Water snakes have relatively long tails, but they aren't especially prehensile. They are primarily used as a paddle and rudder while swimming and as a base of support when crawling on the ground.

Because males carry their hemipenes inside their tail bases, males have proportionately longer and thicker tails than females do.

Internal Organs

Snakes have internal organs that largely mirror those of other vertebrates, except that snakes tend to stagger their paired organs, such as kidneys, testis and ovaries.

The digestive system of snakes is relatively similar to those of vertebrates, featuring an esophagus that accepts food from the mouth and transports it to the stomach, followed by long intestines that transport food from the stomach to the anus where the food residue is expelled. Along the way, the liver, gall bladder, spleen and pancreas aid the digestive process by producing and storing digestive enzymes.

Snakes propel blood through their bodies via a heart and circulatory system. Like most other advanced snakes (including rat snakes, kingsnakes, vipers and elapids), water snakes only have a single functional lung.

Like most other animals, snakes filter their blood and manage their water levels with their kidneys. Snakes produce uric acid as a byproduct of protein synthesis, and expel it through the vent. This uric acid often looks like pieces of chalk, and is not soluble in water.

The nervous system of snakes is largely similar to that of other animals. The brain – which is relatively small – provides the control over the body by sending impulses through the spinal cord and nerves.

One interesting anatomical feature of water snakes (as well as all other snakes) is their flexible windpipe. Known as the glottis, the tube transports air to and from the lungs and resides in the bottom of snakes' mouths. Snakes have the ability to move their glottis in order to breathe while they are swallowing large food items.

Skeletal System

Snakes have elongated bodies, so they have many more vertebrae than most other vertebrates do. Each vertebra attaches to two of the snake's rib bones.

Aside from their vertebrae and ribs, the only other bones water snakes possess are those that make up the skull. Unlike many primitive snakes, water snakes have no vestigial legs or pelvic girdle.

Reproductive Organs

Male water snakes have paired reproductive structures that they hold inside their tail base. The males evert these organs, termed hemipenes (singular: hemipenis), during mating activities and insert them inside the females' cloacas.

Females also have paired reproductive systems, which essentially mirror those of other vertebrates. One key difference is the presence of structures called oviducts. Oviducts hold the male's sperm and accept the ova after they are released from the ovaries during ovulation.

Chapter 2: Biology and Behavior

Water snakes have evolved a number of biological and behavioral adaptations that allow them to survive in their natural habitats. While they share some of these adaptations with their close relatives, others are unique to water snakes.

Locomotion

Water snakes may employ several different methods of locomotion, but they primarily crawl via lateral undulation or rectilinear motion. When climbing, water snakes use a method called concertina motion.

Lateral undulation occurs when snakes bend their bodies back and forth in an "S" shape. On land, this allows their body to grasp small imperfections in the substrate and propel themselves forward. Lateral undulation is also the method by which water snakes swim, although they are pushing against the water instead of the ground. (BC, 1988)

Rectilinear motion occurs when the water snake use a section of their ventral and lateral muscles to swing their ventral scales forward, grip the substrate, and then pull the snake forward. The process allows the snakes to crawl forward in a straight line, however, it is a very slow method of travel.

Concertina motion involves extending the head and neck in the direction of an accessible perch. The head and chin then grip and pull against the perch, which brings the snake's rear body forward.

Shedding

Like other animals, snakes must shed their outer skin layers as they wear out. While mammals do so continuously, snakes shed their entire external layer of skin cells at periodic intervals.

This process may occur as frequently as once every month when snakes are young and growing quickly, or as rarely as two or three times per year for larger, mature snakes.

Snakes that are injured, ill or parasitized may shed more frequently than usual. Some shedding events, such as the snake's first shed, or the females' post-ovulation shed, mark important milestones.

The shedding process takes approximately 7 to 10 days to complete. Initially, the snake begins producing a layer of fluid between the two outermost layers of skin. This serves as a lubricant that helps the old skin to peel off.

After a day or two, this fluid may become visible and give the snakes a cloudy appearance. It is often most apparent when viewing the snake's ventral surface or eyes. Because clear scales cover the eyes of snakes, the fluid makes the eyes of most pre-shed snakes look very cloudy and blue. At this time, the snake's vision is impaired, and most snakes spend this time hiding.

A few days later, the snake's eyes clear up, and it looks normal again. A day or two later, the snake will begin the process of shedding.

Snakes begin the process by trying to cut the old layer of skin on their lips. They do this by rubbing their faces against stationary surfaces. While many keepers incorporate rough surfaces in the cage for fear that the snake will not be able to shed without them, this is rarely a problem in practice. The cage walls are usually more than adequate for the purpose.

After separating the skin on the lips, the old skin starts to peel away. The snake crawls forward, leaving the old skin behind. The fresh, clean new skin usually looks much brighter than it did just a few days earlier.

Metabolism and Digestion
Water snakes are ectothermic ("cold-blooded") animals, whose internal metabolism depends on their internal body temperature. When they are warm, their bodily functions proceed more rapidly; when they are cold, their bodily functions proceed slowly.

This also means that water snakes digest more effectively at suitably warm temperatures than they do at suboptimal temperatures. Their appetites also vary with temperature, and if the temperatures drop below the preferred range, they may cease feeding entirely.

A water snake's body temperature largely follows ambient air temperatures, but they also absorb and reflect radiant heat, such as that coming from the sun.

Growth Rate and Lifespan

Water snakes grow at a fairly rapid rate. Although these growth rates differ from species to species and one population to the next, many wild populations grow between .06 and .13 centimeters per day. (King, 1986)

In practice, most water snakes will grow from about 8 to 12 inches (20 to 30 centimeters) at birth to between 18 and 36 inches (45 to 90 centimeters) by their second birthday. Most will continue to grow after this, although the rate will slow considerably. Water snakes generally reach sexual maturity between 2 and 4 years of age.

Although there has not been a great deal of research about the lifespans of water snakes, they do not appear to live very long, relative to other snakes. The oldest documented northern water snake was just shy of 10 years old when it died. In any case, it is likely that captive water snakes will outlive their wild counterparts.

Foraging Behavior

Water snakes primarily nourish themselves by actively foraging for prey, although they probably also lie in ambush from time to time, and seize prey that passes.

When actively pursuing prey, water snakes may search on both dry land or in the water. They may even climb trees to attain a better view of animals swimming in the water below.

Water snakes primarily find their prey through a combination of their sense of smell and the vomeronasal sense, but vision also play an important part in the final portions of the foraging process.

Once a water snake has located suitable prey, it strikes out and bites the prey with its sharp teeth, thereby preventing the prey's escape. From that point, it simply begins engulfing the animal – it is not constricted or envenomated.

To consume the item, the snake moves it back further into the mouth with movements of the palatine and pterygoid bones. Once in the throat, muscular contractions move the prey into the stomach.

Defensive Strategies and Tactics

The primary way by which water snakes avoid predators is via their cryptic coloration. Additionally, they tend to be most active during periods of low light.

However, this habit of avoiding detection is not infallible, and a combination of avian and mammalian predators locate these snakes from time to time. When this happens, water snakes usually dive into the water. Once under the surface, they are usually safe from most terrestrial predators.

If this doesn't work, or they do not flee quickly enough, they may unleash a litany of defensive behaviors that are aimed at the attacker. This may include hissing, striking and biting, as well as releasing copious amounts of foul-smelling musk, feces and urates.

Reproduction

While the various subspecies and geographic populations likely exhibit variations on the theme, most water snake populations breed during the spring. Some species may also have a secondary breeding period in the fall.

Unlike many other snake species, in which the males are larger than the females, female water snakes are often much larger than males. Additionally, males rarely engage in combat for breeding rights, and several different individuals may simultaneously court the same female.

Scientists describe water snakes as ovoviviparous – they give birth to live young, but unlike most female mammals, who exchange blood with their developing young, water snakes develop inside thin, flexible eggs.

Whereas oviparous snakes only retain these eggs for a relatively short time before covering them in a calcium-based shell and expelling them from the body (where they will keep developing for a period of time), ovoviviparous snakes retain the eggs inside their bodies until the young are ready to hatch. They then give birth (parturition), at which time the soft, membranous eggs burst (some may break free of their eggs before exiting the mother's body).

Like most other live-bearing snakes, water snakes may consume unfertilized ova (and potentially stillborn young) after parturition. They likely do this to both recover wasted calories and to help reduce odors, which may attract predators.

The young likely seek out protected retreats for the next few days. They shed within about 6 to 12 days of parturition, and begin pursuing food.

Chapter 3: Classification and Taxonomy

North American water snakes of the genus *Nerodia* are a relatively well-defined group of snakes, who all spring from a common ancestor. While the taxonomy of several species and subspecies within the group have been revised several times, the group's basic structure is not in doubt.

But before delving more deeply into the classification and taxonomy of water snakes, it is helpful to begin with a broader context.

Like all other snakes, water snakes are members of the Order Squamata and the Suborder Serpentes. They sit alongside the kingsnakes (*Lampropeltis* spp.), rat snakes (*Pantherophis* spp.) and racers (*Coluber* spp.) in the family Colubridae. Along with the garter snakes (*Thamnophis* spp.) and brown snakes (*Storeria* spp.), water snakes form the Subfamily Natricinae.

As currently construed, the genus *Nerodia* contains nine different species:

- Banded water snake (*Nerodia fasciata*)

- Brazos water snake (*Nerodia harteri*)

- Brown water snake (*Nerodia taxispilota*)

- Concho water snake (*Nerodia paucimaculata*)

- Diamondback water snake (*Nerodia rhombifer*)

- Green water snake (*Nerodia cyclopion*)

- Northern water snake (*Nerodia sipedon*)

- Plainbelly water snake (*Nerodia erythrogaster*)

  - Salt marsh water snake (*Nerodia clarkii*)

Additionally, some authorities split the green water snake into two species: the green water snake (*Nerodia cyclopion*) and the Florida water snake (*Nerodia floridana*).

Different authorities recognize varying numbers of subspecies within many of these species. Some, such as several plainbelly water snake subspecies, are widely recognized, while others do not benefit from such broad consensus.

In most respects, these differences are not critically important to beginning hobbyists.

Chapter 4: The Water Snake's World

To maintain a water snake successfully, you must understand the animal's native habitat and provide a reasonable facsimile of it.

Range

Taken as a group, water snakes of the genus Nerodia inhabit most of the eastern and central United States. Northern water snakes range as far north as Ontario and Quebec, while Brazos water snakes and diamondback water snakes are found as far south as Texas. They are found from the marshes bordering the Atlantic in the east to Colorado in the west.

Climate

The climate water snakes experience is largely dictated by their geographic location.

Temperatures in the northern portion of their range frequently drop below freezing (and remain there for extended periods of time), while summer highs hover in the high 80s to low 90s Fahrenheit (31 to 33 degrees Celsius).

Those living in the northern portions of the United States or in southern Canada experience a very brief active season, stretching from about May to October, while those living in South Florida remain active year-round.

Rainfall and other forms of precipitation vary as well. Generally speaking, those snakes living along the east coast (particularly in the southeast) experience more rainfall each year than those living further west. In some locations, rainfall tends to be spread out relatively evenly throughout the year, while other areas experience more well-defined rainy and dry seasons.

Habitat

Different water snake species prefer slightly different habitats, although all are typically found near some major water source.

Brown, diamondback and blotched water snakes tend to prefer large water bodies, including rivers and lakes. On the other hand, plain-belly water snakes are most commonly associated with wetland environments. Slat marsh water snakes are frequently found near the coast, and occasionally inhabit brackish marshes.

Northern water snakes are perhaps the most flexible of all species, and they can be found in virtually any habitat that contains water. This not only includes ponds, lakes, creeks, rivers and streams, but also swamps, beaver ponds, backyard ponds and drainage ditches.

Natural Diet

Most water snakes are relatively opportunistic feeders, who will eagerly capture and consume virtually any small creature they encounter. However, a few species exhibit definite preferences.

For example, northern water snakes may consume a dozen different foods over the course of their lives, while plain-belly water snakes typically prefer frogs and tadpoles to all other prey. Brown water snakes, on the other hand, prefer catfish to most other fish species.

Some of the most common prey types eaten by water snakes include:

- Fish

- Frogs and tadpoles

- Salamanders

- Smaller snakes

- Large aquatic invertebrates

- Crayfish

- Turtles

- Eggs

- Rodents

Natural Predators

A wide variety of large and medium-sized predators routinely prey upon water snakes – particularly juveniles. Some of the most important predators include:

- Other water snakes

- Kingsnakes

- Cottonmouths

- Herons and other wading birds

- Raccoons

- Minks and otters

- Large turtles

- Large frogs

- Owls

- Hawks

- Crows and jays

- Opossums

- Alligators

- Large fish

- Large invertebrates

PART II: WATER SNAKE HUSBANDRY

Once equipped with a basic understanding of what water snakes *are* (Chapter 1 and Chapter 3), where they *live* (Chapter 4), and what they *do* (Chapter 2) you can begin learning about their captive care.

Animal husbandry is an evolving pursuit. Keepers shift their strategies frequently as they incorporate new information and ideas into their husbandry paradigms.

There are few "right" or "wrong" answers, and what works in one situation may not work in another. Accordingly, you may find that different authorities present different, and sometimes conflicting, information regarding the care of these snakes.

In all cases, you must strive to learn as much as you can about your pet and its natural habitat, so that you may provide it with the best quality of life possible.

Chapter 5: Water Snakes as Pets

Water snakes can make rewarding pets, but you must know what to expect before adding one to your home and family. This includes not only understanding the nature of the care they require, but also the costs associated with this care.

Assuming that you feel confident in your ability to care for a snake and endure the associated financial burdens, you can begin seeking your individual pet.

Understanding the Commitment

Keeping a water snake as a pet requires a substantial commitment. You will be responsible for your pet's well-being for the rest of its life. Although water snakes are not particularly long-lived animals, their lifespans are not trivial.

Can you be sure that you will still want to care for your pet several years in the future? Do you know what your living situation will be? What changes will have occurred in your family? How will your working life have changed over this time?

You must consider all of these possibilities before acquiring a new pet. Failing to do so often leads to apathy, neglect and even resentment, which is not good for you or your pet snake.

Neglecting your pet is wrong, and in some locations, a criminal offense. You must continue to provide quality care for your snake, even once the novelty has worn off, and it is no longer fun to clean the cage and purchase fish and frogs a few times a week.

Once you purchase a water snake, its well-being becomes your responsibility until it passes away at the end of a long life, or you have found someone who will agree to adopt the animal for you. Unfortunately, this is rarely an easy task. You may begin with thoughts of selling your pet to help recoup a small part of your investment, but these efforts will largely fall flat.

While professional breeders may profit from the sale of water snakes, amateurs are at a decided disadvantage. Only a tiny sliver of the general population is interested in reptilian pets, and only a small subset of these are interested in keeping water snakes.

Of those who are interested in acquiring a water snake, most would rather start fresh, by *purchasing* a juvenile from an established breeder, rather than adopting your questionable animal *for free.*

After having difficulty finding a willing party to purchase or adopt your animal, many owners try to donate their pet to a local zoo. Unfortunately, this rarely works either.

Zoos are not interested in your pet water snake, no matter how pretty he is and how tame he is when you hold him. He is a pet with little to no reliable provenance and questionable health status. This is simply not the type of animal zoos are eager to add to their multi-million dollar collections.

Zoos obtain most of their animals from other zoos and museums; failing that, they obtain their animals directly from their land of origin. As a rule, they do not accept donated pets.

No matter how difficult it becomes to find a new home for your unwanted water snake, you must never release non-native reptiles into the wild. Reptiles can colonize places outside their native range, with disastrous results for the ecosystem's native fauna.

Additionally, released or escaped reptiles cause a great deal of distress to those who are frightened by them. This leads local municipalities to adopt pet restrictions or ban reptile keeping entirely.

While the chances of an escaped or released water snake harming anyone are very low, it is unlikely that those who fear reptiles will see the threat as minor.

The Costs of Captivity

Reptiles are often marketed as low-cost pets. While true in a relative sense (the costs associated with dog, cat, horse or tropical fish husbandry are often much higher than they are for water snakes), potential keepers must still prepare for the financial implications of water snake ownership.

At the outset, you must budget for the acquisition of your pet, as well as the costs of purchasing or constructing a habitat. Unfortunately, while many keepers plan for these costs, they typically fail to consider the on-going costs, which will quickly eclipse the initial startup costs.

Startup Costs
One surprising fact most new keepers learn is the enclosure and equipment will often cost more than the animal does (except in the case of very high-priced specimens).

Prices fluctuate from one market to the next, but in general, the least you will spend on a healthy water snake is about $25 (£20), while the least you will spend on the *initial* habitat and assorted equipment will be about $50 (£40). Replacement equipment and food will represent additional (and ongoing) expenses.

Examine the charts on the following pages to get an idea of three different pricing scenarios. While the specific prices listed will vary based on innumerable factors, the charts are instructive for first-time buyers.

The first scenario details a budget-minded keeper, trying to spend as little as possible. The second example estimates the costs for a keeper with a moderate budget, and the third example provides a case study for extravagant shoppers, who want an expensive water snake and top-notch equipment.

These charts are only provided estimates; your experience may vary based on a variety of factors.

A diamondback water snake.

27

Inexpensive Option

Wild Caught Water Snake	$25 (£20)
Economy Homemade Habitat	$25 (£20)
Heat Lamp Fixture and Bulbs	$20 (£16)
Plants, Substrate, Hides, etc.	$20 (£16)
Infrared Thermometer	$35 (£24)
Digital Indoor-Outdoor Thermometer	$20 (£16)
Water Dish, Forceps, Spray Bottles, Misc.	$20 (£16)
Total	**$165 (£128)**

Moderate Option

Captive Bred Water Snake	$50 (£40)
Premium Homemade Habitat	$100 (£80)
Heat Lamp Fixture and Bulbs	$20 (£16)
Plants, Substrate, Hides, etc.	$20 (£16)
Infrared Thermometer	$35 (£24)
Digital Indoor-Outdoor Thermometer	$20 (£16)
Water Dish, Forceps, Spray Bottles, Misc.	$20 (£16)
Total	**$265 (£208)**

Premium Option

Designer Water Snake	$500 (£400)
Premium Commercial Cage	$200 (£160)
Heat Lamp Fixture and Bulbs	$20 (£16)
Plants, Substrate, Hides, etc.	$20 (£16)
Infrared Thermometer	$35 (£24)
Digital Indoor-Outdoor Thermometer	$20 (£16)
Water Dish, Forceps, Spray Bottles, Misc.	$20 (£16)
Total	**$815 (£648)**

Ongoing Costs

The ongoing costs of water snake ownership primarily fall into one of three categories: food, maintenance and veterinary care.

Food costs are the most significant of the three, but they are relatively consistent and somewhat predictable. Some maintenance costs are easy to calculate, but things like equipment malfunctions are impossible to predict with any certainty. Veterinary expenses are hard to predict and vary wildly from one year to the next.

Food Costs

Food is the single greatest ongoing cost you will experience while caring for your water snake. To obtain a reasonable estimate of your yearly food costs, you must consider the number of meals you will feed your pet per year and the cost of each meal.

The amount of food your water snake will consume will vary based on numerous factors, including his size, the average temperatures in his habitat and his health.

As a ballpark number, you should figure that you'll need about $5 to $10 (£4 to £8) per week – roughly $250 to $500 (£205 to £410) per year -- for food. You could certainly spend more or less than this, but that is a reasonable estimate for back-of-the-envelope calculations.

Veterinary Costs

While you should always seek veterinary advice at the first sign of illness, it is probably not wise to haul your healthy water snake to the vet's office for no reason – they don't require "checkups" or annual vaccinations as some other pets may. Accordingly, you shouldn't incur any veterinary expenses unless your pet falls ill.

However, veterinary care can become very expensive, very quickly. In addition to a basic exam or phone consultation, your snake may need cultures, x-rays or other diagnostic tests performed. In light of this, wise keepers budget at least $200 to $300 (£160 to £245) each year to cover any emergency veterinary costs.

Maintenance Costs

It is important to plan for both routine and unexpected maintenance costs. Commonly used items, such as paper towels, disinfectant and top soil are rather easy to calculate. However, it is not easy to know how many burned out light bulbs, cracked misting units or faulty thermostats you will have to replace in a given year.

Those who keep their water snake in simple enclosures will find that about $50 (£40) covers their yearly maintenance costs. By contrast, those who maintain elaborate habitats may spend $200 (£160) or more each year.

Always try to purchase frequently used supplies, such as light bulbs, paper towels and disinfectants in bulk to maximize your savings. It is often beneficial to consult with local reptile-keeping clubs, who often pool their resources to attain greater buying power.

Myths and Misunderstandings

Snakes are the subject for countless myths and misunderstandings. It is important to rectify any flawed perceptions before welcoming one into your life.

Myth: Snakes grow in proportion to the size of their cage and then stop.

Fact: Snakes do no such thing. Healthy snakes grow throughout their lives, although the rate of growth slows with age. Placing them in a small cage in an attempt to stunt their growth is an unthinkably cruel practice, which is more likely to sicken or kill the snake than stunt its growth.

Myth: Snakes can sense fear.

Fact: Snakes are not magical creatures. They are constrained by physics and biology just as humans, dogs and squid are. With that said, it is possible for some animals to read human body language very well. Some long-time keepers have noticed differences in the behavior of some snakes when people of varying comfort levels handle them. This difference in behavior may be confused with the snake "sensing fear."

Myth: Snakes must eat live food.

Fact: While snakes primarily hunt live prey in the wild, a few species consume carrion when the opportunity presents itself. In captivity, most snakes learn to accept dead prey. Whenever possible, hobbyists should feed dead prey to their snakes to minimize the suffering of the prey animal and reduce the chances that the snake will become injured.

Myth: Snakes have no emotions and do not suffer.

Fact: While snakes have very primitive brains, and do not have emotions comparable to those of higher mammals, they can absolutely suffer. Always treat snakes with the same compassion you would offer a dog, cat or horse.

Myth: Snakes prefer elaborately decorated cages that resemble their natural habitat.

Fact: While some snakes thrive better in complex habitats that offer a variety of hiding and thermoregulatory options, they do not appreciate your aesthetic efforts.

Unlike humans, who experience the world through their eyes, snakes experience the world largely as they perceive it through their vomeronasal system. Your water snake is not impressed with the rainforest wallpaper decorating the walls of his cage.

Additionally, while many snakes require hiding spaces, they do not seem to mind whether this hiding space is in the form of a rock, a rotten log or a paper plate. As long as the hiding spot is safe and snug, they will utilize it.

Myth: All water snakes are mean animals, who will always bite their keeper.

Fact: Many water snakes are, in fact, rather defensive. However, there are plenty of exceptions to this rule, and many who are raised in captivity from a young age learn to tolerate interaction with their keepers over time.

Acquiring Your Water Snake

Modern reptile enthusiasts can acquire water snakes from a variety of sources, each with a different set of pros and cons.

Pet stores are one of the first places many people see water snakes, and they become the de facto source of pets for many beginning keepers. While they do offer some unique benefits to prospective keepers, pet stores are not always the best place to purchase a snake; so, consider all of the available options, including breeders and reptile swap meets, before making a purchase.

Pet Stores

Pet stores offer a number of benefits to keepers shopping for water snakes, including convenience: They usually stock all of the equipment your new snake needs, including cages, heating devices and food items.

Additionally, they offer you the chance to inspect the snake up close before purchase. In some cases, you may be able to choose from more than one specimen. Many pet stores provide health guarantees for a short period, that provides some recourse if your new pet turns out to be ill.

However, pet stores are not always the ideal place to purchase your new pet. Pet stores are retail establishments, and as such, you will usually pay more for your new pet than you would from a breeder.

Additionally, pet stores rarely know the pedigree of the animals they sell, and they will rarely know the snake's date of birth, or other pertinent information.

Other drawbacks associated with pet stores primarily relate to the staff's inexperience. While some pet stores concentrate on reptiles and may educate their staff about proper water snake care, many others provide incorrect advice to their customers.

It is also worth considering the increased exposure to pathogens that pet store animals endure, given the constant flow of animals through such facilities.

Reptile Expos

Reptile expos offer another option for purchasing a water snake. Reptile expos often feature resellers, breeders and retailers in the same room, all selling various types of snakes and other reptiles.

Often, the prices at such events are quite reasonable and you are often able to select from many different snakes. However, if you have a problem, it may be difficult to find the seller after the event is over.

Breeders
Because they usually offer unparalleled information and support to their customers, breeders are generally the best place for most novices to shop for water snakes. Additionally, breeders often know the species well, and are better able to help you learn the husbandry techniques necessary for success.

For those seeking a particular type of water snake, breeders are often the only option. You won't find many albino water snakes in many pet stores, for example.

The primary disadvantage of buying from a breeder is that you must often make such purchases from a distance, either by phone or via the internet. Nevertheless, most established breeders are happy to provide you with photographs of the animal you will be purchasing, as well as his or her parents.

Selecting Your Water Snake
Not all water snakes are created equally, so it is important to select a healthy individual that will give you the best chance of success.

Practically speaking, the most important criterion to consider is the health of the animal. However, the sex, age and history of the snake are also important things to consider.

Health Checklist
Always check your water snake thoroughly for signs of injury or illness before purchasing it. If you are purchasing the animal from someone in a different part of the country, you must inspect it immediately upon delivery. Notify the seller promptly if the animal exhibits any health problems.

Avoid the temptation to acquire or accept a sick or injured animal in hopes of nursing him back to health. Not only are you likely to incur substantial veterinary costs while treating your new pet, you will likely fail in your attempts to restore the lizard to full health. Sick water snakes rarely recover in the hands of novices.

Additionally, by purchasing injured or diseased animals, you incentivize poor husbandry on the part of the retailer. If retailers lose money on sick or injured animals, they will take steps to avoid this eventuality, by acquiring healthier stock in the first place, and providing better care for their charges.

As much as is possible, try to observe the following features:

- **Observe the snake's skin**. It should be free of lacerations and other damage. Pay special attention to those areas that frequently sustain damage, such as the tip of the tail and the snout. A small cut or abrasion may be relatively easy to treat, but significant abrasions and cuts are likely to become infected and require significant treatment.

- **Gently check the snake's crevices and creases for mites and ticks**. Mites are about the size of a flake of pepper, and they may be black, brown or red. Mites often move about on the lizard, whereas ticks – if attached and feeding – do not move. Avoid purchasing any animal that has either parasite. Additionally, you should avoid purchasing any other animals from this source, as they are likely to harbor parasites as well.

- **Examine the snake's eyes and nostrils**. The eyes should not be sunken, and they should be free of discharge. The nostrils should be clear and dry – snakes with runny noses or those who blow bubbles are likely to be suffering from a respiratory infection. However, be aware that water snakes often get some water in their nostrils while drinking water. This is no cause for concern.

- **Gently palpate the animal and ensure no lumps or anomalies are apparent**. Lumps in the muscles or abdominal cavity may indicate parasites, abscesses or tumors.

- **Observe the snake's demeanor**. Healthy snakes are aware of their environment and react to stimuli. When active, the snake should calmly explore his environment. While you may wish to avoid purchasing an aggressive, defensive or flighty animal, these behaviors do not necessarily indicate a health problem.

- **Check the snake's vent**. The vent should be clean and free of smeared feces. Smeared feces can indicate parasites or bacterial infections.

- **Check the snake's appetite**. If possible, ask the retailer to feed the water snake in front of you. A healthy water snake should usually exhibit a strong food drive, although failing to eat is not *necessarily* a bad sign – the animal may not be hungry.

The Age
Neonatal water snakes are very fragile until they reach about one or two months of age. Before this, they are unlikely to thrive in the hands of beginning keepers.

Accordingly, most beginners should purchase animals that are at least 3 or 4 months old. Animals of this age tolerate the changes associated with a new home better than very young specimens do. Further, given their greater size, they will better tolerate temperature and humidity extremes than smaller animals will.

The Sex
Unless you are attempting to breed water snakes, you should select a male pet, as females are more likely to suffer from reproduction-related health problems than males are.

Quarantine
Because new animals may have illnesses or parasites that could infect the rest of your collection, it is wise to quarantine all new acquisitions. This means that you should keep any new animal as separated from the rest of your pets as possible. Only once you have ensured that the new animal is healthy should you introduce it to the rest of your collection.

During the quarantine period, you should keep the new snake in a simplified habitat, with a paper substrate, water bowl, basking spot and a few hiding places. Keep the temperature and humidity at ideal levels.

It is wise to obtain fecal samples from your snake during the quarantine period. You can take these samples to your veterinarian, who can check them for signs of internal parasites. Always treat any existing parasite infestations before removing the animal from quarantine.

Always tend to quarantined animals last, as this reduces the chances of transmitting pathogens to your healthy animals. Do not wash quarantined water bowls or cage furniture with those belonging to your healthy animals. Whenever possible, use completely separate tools for quarantined animals and those that have been in your collection for some time.

Always be sure to wash your hands thoroughly after handling quarantined animals, their cages or their tools. Particularly careful keepers wear a smock or alternative clothing when handling quarantined animals.

A midland water snake.

Quarantine new acquisitions for a minimum of 30 days; 60 or 90 days is even better. Many zoos and professional breeders maintain 180- or 360-day-long quarantine periods.

Chapter 6: Providing the Captive Habitat

In most respects, providing water snakes with a suitable captive habitat requires that you functionally replicate the various aspects of their wild habitats.

In addition to providing your pet with an enclosure, you must provide the animal with the correct thermal environment, appropriate humidity, substrate, and suitable cage furniture.

Enclosure

Providing your water snake with appropriate housing is and essential aspect of captive care. In essence, the habitat you provide to your pet becomes his world.

In the "old days," those inclined to keep reptiles had few choices with regard to caging. The two primary options were to build a custom cage from scratch or construct a lid to use with a fish aquarium.

By contrast, modern hobbyists have a variety of options from which to choose. In addition to building custom cages or adapting aquaria, dozens of different enclosure styles are available – each with different pros and cons.

Remember: There are few absolutes regarding reptile husbandry. What works for most keepers and snakes may not work for you and your pet. Additionally, advanced keepers are often able to sidestep problems that trouble beginners.

Dimensions

Throughout their lives, snakes need a cage large enough to lay comfortably, access a range of temperatures and get enough room for exercise.

The rule of thumb for most snakes is to ensure that the animal is no longer than ½ the length of the cage's perimeter.

Generally speaking, this means that hatchlings and young snakes require about 1 to 2 square feet of space (0.10 to 0.20 square meters). Large, mature animals require about 6 to 8 square feet (0.5 to 0.75

square meters) of space, although some keepers offer slightly more or less than this.

While water snake are frequently found climbing in the wild, they do not require very tall cages. Even large adults will thrive in cages with 18 to 24 inches (45 to 60 centimeters) of height – more than this will cause heating challenges.

In addition to total space, the layout of the cage is also important – rectangular cages are strongly preferable to square, round or octagonal cages for a variety of reasons:

-They allow the keeper to establish better thermal gradients.

-Cages with one long direction allow your snake to stretch out better than square cages do.

-If the cage is accessible via front-opening doors, you will not have to reach as far back in a rectangular cage as you would a square cage when cleaning.

Aquariums
Aquariums are popular choices for snake cages, largely because of their ubiquity. Virtually any pet store that carries snakes also stocks aquariums.

Aquariums can make suitable snake cages, but they have a number of drawbacks.

-Aquariums (and other glass cages) are hard to clean

-Aquariums are very fragile

-Aquariums do not retain heat very well

-Aquariums require an after-market or custom built lid

-Aquariums often develop water spots from repeated mistings

When aquariums are used with screened tops, the excess ventilation may cause the tank to dry out rapidly. This can be a challenge for water snake keepers, who are attempting to keep their cages relatively humid. To work around this, some keepers attach plastic or glass covers over a portion of the screened lid.

Commercial Cages

Commercially produced cages have a number of benefits over other enclosures. Commercial cages usually feature doors on the front of the cage, which provide better access than top-opening cages do. Additionally, bypass glass doors or framed, hinged doors are generally more secure than after-market screened lids are.

Plastic cages are usually produced in dimensions that make more sense for snakes, and often have features that aid in heating and lighting the cage.

Commercial cages can be made out of wood, metal, glass or other substances, but the majority are made from PVC or ABS plastic.

Commercial cages are available in two primary varieties: those that are molded from one piece of plastic and those that are assembled from several different sheets. Assembled cages are less expensive and easier to construct, but molded cages have few (if any) seams or cracks in which bacteria and fungus can thrive.

Some cage manufacturers produce cages in multiple colors. White is probably the best color for novices, as it is easy to see dirt, mites and other small problems. A single mite crawling on a white cage surface is very visible, even from a distance.

Black cages do not show dirt as well. Such cages are most appropriate for more experienced keepers who have developed proper hygiene techniques over time.

Plastic Storage Containers

Plastic storage containers, such as those used for shoes, sweaters or food, make suitable cages for small water snakes. However, the lids for plastic storage boxes are rarely secure enough for use with snakes.

Hobbyists and breeders overcome this by incorporating Velcro straps, hardware latches or other strategies into plastic storage container cages.

The best way to use plastic storage containers is with a wooden or plastic rack. Such systems are often designed to use containers without lids. In these "lidless" systems, the shelves of the rack form the top to the cage sitting below them. The gap between the top of the sides of the storage containers and the bottom of the shelves is usually very tight – approximately one-eighth inch (2 millimeters) or less.

When plastic containers are used, you must drill or melt numerous holes for air exchange. If you are using a lid, it is acceptable to place the holes in the lid; however, if you are using a lidless system, you will have to make the holes in the sides of the boxes.

Drill or melt all of the holes from the inside of the box, towards the outside of the box. This will help reduce the chances of leaving sharp edges inside the cage, which could cut the snake.

If you intend to heat a single plastic storage box with a heat lamp, you will need to cut a hole in the lid, and cover the hole with hardware cloth or screen. Attach the mesh or hardware cloth with silicone or cable ties. You can now place the heat lamp on top of the mesh.

Homemade Cages
For keepers with access to tools and the desire and skill to use them, it is possible to construct homemade cages.

A number of materials are suitable for cage construction, and each has different pros and cons. Wood is commonly used, but must be adequately sealed to avoid rotting, warping or absorbing offensive odors.

Plastic sheeting is a very good material, but few have the necessary skills, knowledge and tools necessary for cage construction. Additionally, some plastics may have extended off-gassing times.

Glass can be used, whether glued to itself or when used with a frame. Custom-built glass cages can be better than aquariums, as you can design them in dimensions that are appropriate for snakes. Additionally, they can be constructed in such a way that the door is on the front of the cage, rather than the top.

Regardless of the materials used, security and safety are of paramount importance when constructing a custom cage.

Screen Cages

Screen cages make excellent habitats for some lizards and frogs, but they are not suitable for water snakes. Screened cages do not retain heat well, and they are hard to keep suitably humid.

Additionally, screen cages are difficult to clean and often develop weak spots that can give the inhabitant enough of a hole to push through and escape.

Chapter 7: Establishing the Thermal Environment

Providing the proper thermal environment is one of the most important aspects of reptile husbandry. As ectothermic ("cold blooded") animals, water snakes rely on the local temperatures to regulate the rate at which their metabolism operates.

Snakes deprived of access to suitable temperatures spend a great deal of time at the veterinarian's office, battling infections and illness. Accordingly, you must provide your pet with an appropriate thermal environment.

This requires you to understand the temperature range appropriate for water snakes, the correct techniques for achieving such temperatures, and the equipment needed to do so.

Preferred Temperatures for Water Snakes

Although different water snake species sometimes demonstrate slightly different preferences, most water snakes prefer ambient daytime temperatures in the low 80s Fahrenheit (about 26 to 27 degrees Celsius), although the require access to a basking spot of about 90 degrees Fahrenheit (32 degrees Celsius). At night, they prefer a slight drop in temperature; the high 60s to low 70s Fahrenheit (20 to 22 degrees Celsius) are ideal.

However, it is important to understand that your snake's body size influences these preferences. Because volume increases more quickly than surface area does with increasing body size, small individuals experience more rapid temperature fluctuations than larger individuals do.

This kind of thermal stress affects small snakes quickly, and excessively high or low temperatures may prove fatal. Accordingly, it is wise to avoid temperature extremes with young water snakes.

Thermal Gradients

In their natural habitat, water snakes can keep their bodies within these preferred ranges by altering their behavior. For example, a wild water snake who is trying to digest a large meal may bask on a sunny rock. Conversely, the same snake may retreat into a rodent burrow later that day, to avoid oppressive heat.

You want to provide similar opportunities for your captive snake by creating a thermal gradient.

The best way to do this is by clustering the heating devices at one end of the habitat, thereby creating a basking spot (the warmest spot in the enclosure).

Because no heating devices are placed at the opposite end of the cage, the temperature will slowly drop with increasing distance from the basking spot. This arrangement creates a *gradient* of temperatures.

By establishing a gradient in the enclosure, your snake will be able to access a range of different temperatures. This will allow him to manage his body temperature just as his wild counterparts do.

Adjust the heating device until the surface temperatures at the basking spot are about 90 degrees Fahrenheit (32 degrees Celsius). Ambient temperatures at the basking spot should be in the high 80s Fahrenheit (30 to 31 degrees Celsius). Provide a slightly cooler basking spot for small individuals, with maximum surface temperatures of about 88 degrees Fahrenheit (31 degrees Celsius).

Ideally, the cool end of the cage should be in the low 70s Fahrenheit (22 to 23 degrees Celsius) during the day, when the heat source is on.

This range of temperatures will allow your snake to maintain his body temperature at the preferred level, somewhere in the middle of this range.

The need to establish a thermal gradient is one of the most compelling reasons to use a large cage. In general, the larger the cage, the easier it is to establish a suitable thermal gradient.

Heating Equipment
A variety of heating devices are available to water snake keepers. Each has its own set of pros and cons, so wise keepers consider the decision carefully before deciding which type of heat source to use.

Heat Lamps

Heat lamps are one of the best choices for supplying heat to water snakes. Heat lamps consist of a reflector dome and an incandescent bulb. The light bulb produces heat (in addition to light) and the metal reflector dome directs the heat to a spot inside the cage.

If you use a cage with a metal screen lid, you can rest the reflector dome directly on the screen; otherwise, you will need to clamp the lamp to something over the cage. Always be sure that the lamp will not be dislodged by vibration, children or pets.

In the interest of fire safety, it is wise to opt for heavy-duty reflector domes with ceramic bases, rather than economy units with plastic bases.

While you can use specialized light bulbs that are designed for use with reptiles, they are not necessary. Regular, economy, incandescent bulbs work well. Snakes do not require special lighting, and incandescent bulbs – even those produced for use with reptiles – rarely generate much UVA, and never generate UVB.

One of the greatest benefits of using heat lamps to maintain the temperature of your snake's habitat is the inherent (and affordable) flexibility with these types of heating devices.

Heat lamps offer flexibility in two ways:

Changing the Bulb Wattage

The simplest way to adjust the temperature of your snake's cage is by changing the wattage of the bulb being used. For example, if a 40-watt light bulb is not raising the temperature of the basking spot high enough, you may try a 60-watt bulb. Alternatively, if a 100-watt light bulb is elevating the cage temperatures higher than are appropriate, switching the bulb to a 60-watt model may help.

Adjusting the Height of the Heat Lamp

The closer the heat lamp is to the cage, the warmer the cage will be; so, use this principle to your advantage. For example, if the habitat is too warm, the light can be raised, which should lower the cage temperatures slightly.

However, the higher the heat lamp is raised, the larger the basking spot becomes. Accordingly, it is important to be careful that you do not raise the light too high, which results in reducing the effectiveness of the cage's thermal gradient. In very large cages, this may not compromise the thermal gradient very much, but in a small cage, it may eliminate the "cool side" of the habitat entirely.

In other words, if your heat lamp creates a basking spot that is roughly 1-foot in diameter when it rests directly on the screen, it may produce a slightly cooler, but larger basking spot when raised 6-inches above the level of the screen.

Ceramic Heat Emitters
Ceramic heat emitters are small inserts that function similarly to light bulbs, except that they do not produce any visible light – they only produce infrared radiation (heat).

Ceramic heat emitters are used in reflector-dome fixtures, just as heat lamps are. The benefits of such devices are numerous:

-They typically last much longer than light bulbs do

-They are suitable for use with thermostats

-They allow for the creation of overhead basking spots, as lights do

-They can be used day or night

However, the devices do have three primary drawbacks:

-They are very hot when in operation

-They are much more expensive than light bulbs

-You cannot tell by looking if they are hot or cool. This can be a safety hazard – touching a ceramic heat emitter while it is hot is likely to cause serious burns.

Radiant Heat Panels
Quality radiant heat panels are the best choice for heating most reptile habitats, including those containing water snakes.

Radiant heat panels are essentially heat pads that are attached to the roof of the habitat. They usually feature plastic or metal casings and internal reflectors to direct the heat back into the cage.

Radiant heat panels have a number of benefits over traditional heat lamps and under tank heat pads:

-They do not contact the animal at all, thus reducing the risk of burns.

-They do not produce visible light, which means they are useful for both diurnal and nocturnal heat production. They can be used in conjunction with fluorescent light fixtures during the day, and remain on at night once the lights go off.

-They are inherently flexible. Unlike many devices that do not work well with pulse-proportional thermostats, most radiant heat panels work well with on-off and pulse-proportional thermostats.

The only real drawback to radiant heat panels is their cost: radiant heat panels often cost about two to three times the price of light- or heat pad-oriented systems.

However, many radiant heat panels outlast light bulbs and heat pads, a fact that offsets their high initial cost over the long term.

Heat Pads
Heat pads are an attractive option for many keepers, but they are not without drawbacks.

-Heat pads can cause contact burns.

-If they malfunction, they can damage the cage as well as the surface on which they are placed.

-They are more likely to cause a fire than heat lamps or radiant heat panels are.

However, if installed properly (which includes allowing fresh air to flow over the exposed side of the heat pad) and used in conjunction with a thermostat, they can be reasonably safe.

When using heat pads, it is especially important to purchase premium products, which are usually safer than their cheaper counterparts, despite the small increase in price.

Heat Tape

Heat tape is somewhat akin to "stripped down" heat pads. In fact, most heat pads are simply pieces of heat tape that have already been connected and sealed inside a plastic envelope.

Heat tape is primarily used to heat large numbers of cages simultaneously. It is generally inappropriate for novices, and requires the keeper to make electrical connections. Additionally, a thermostat is always required when using heat tape.

Historically, heat tape was used to keep water pipes from freezing – not to heat reptile cages. While some commercial heat tapes have been designed specifically for reptiles, many have not. Accordingly, it may be illegal, not to mention dangerous, to use heat tapes that are not specifically designed for reptile-related applications.

Heat Cables

Heat cables are similar to heat tape, in that they heat a long strip of the cage, but they are much more flexible and easy to use. Many heat cables are suitable to use inside the cage, while others are designed for use outside the habitat.

Always be sure to purchase heat cables that are designed specifically for reptile cages. Those sold at hardware stores are not appropriate for use in snake cages.

Heat cables must be used in conjunction with a thermostat, or, at the very least, a rheostat.

Heated Rocks

In the early days of commercial reptile products, faux rocks, branches and caves with internal heating elements were very popular. However, they have generally fallen out of favor among modern keepers. These rocks and branches were often made with poor craftsmanship and cheap materials, causing them to fail and produce tragic results. Additionally, many keepers used the rocks improperly, leading to injuries, illnesses and death for many unfortunate reptiles.

Heated rocks are not designed to heat an entire cage; they are designed to provide a localized source of heat for the reptile.

Nevertheless, many keepers tried to use them as the primary heat source for the cage, resulting in dangerously cool cage temperatures.

When snakes must rely on small, localized heat sources placed in otherwise chilly cages, they often hug these heat sources for extended periods of time. This can lead to serious thermal burns – whether or not the unit functions properly. This illustrates the key reason why these devices make adequate supplemental heat sources, but they should not be used as primary heating sources.

Modern hot rocks utilize better features, materials and craftsmanship than the old models did, but they still offer few benefits to the keeper or the kept. Additionally, any heating devices that are designed to be used inside the cage necessitate passing an electric cable through a hole, which is not always easy to accomplish. However, some cages do feature passageways for chords.

Room Heat
Some keepers with very large collections elect to heat the entire room, rather than individual cages. While this is an economic and viable solution for advanced keepers, it is not appropriate for novices.

Heating the whole room, instead of an individual cage, makes it very difficult to achieve a good thermal gradient. Experienced keepers may be able to maintain their snakes successfully in this manner, but beginners should always rely on the added safety afforded by a gradient.

Additionally, room heat is rarely cost-effective for a keeper with a pet snake or two. Relying on a single heating source for an entire room is also a high-risk proposition; if the heater or thermostat fails in the "on" position, the entire room may overheat.

Thermometers
It is important to monitor the cage temperatures very carefully to ensure your pet stays health. Just as a water test kit is an aquarist's best friend, quality thermometers are some of the most important husbandry tools for reptile keepers.

Two different types of temperature are relevant for pet snakes: **ambient temperatures** and **surface temperatures**.

The ambient temperature in your animal's enclosure is the air temperature; the surface temperatures are the temperatures of the objects in the cage. Both are important to monitor, as they can differ widely.

For example, the air temperatures may be 90 degrees Fahrenheit (32 degrees Celsius) outside on a hot summer day, but the surface of a black rock may be in excess of 120 degrees Fahrenheit (49 degrees Celsius).

The differences between ambient and surface temperatures can significantly affect your snake's health. For example, surface temperatures of 120 degrees Fahrenheit (49 degrees Celsius) may burn your animal, but they may not kill your pet. Conversely, ambient temperatures in this range will quickly prove fatal.

Measure the cage's ambient temperatures with a digital thermometer. An indoor-outdoor model will feature a probe that allows you to measure the temperature at both ends of the thermal gradient at once. For example, you may position the thermometer at the cool side of the cage, but attach the remote probe to a branch near the basking spot.

Because standard digital thermometers do not measure surface temperatures well, use a non-contact, infrared thermometer for such measurements. These devices will allow you to measure surface temperatures accurately from a short distance away.

Thermal Control Equipment

Some heating devices, such as heat lamps, are designed to operate at full capacity for the entire time that they are turned on. Such devices should not be used with thermostats – instead, care should be taken to calibrate the proper temperature.

Other devices, such as heat pads, heat tape and radiant heat panels are designed to be used with a regulating device to maintain the proper temperature, such as a thermostat or rheostat.

Rheostats

Rheostats are similar to light-dimmer switches, and they allow you to reduce the output of a heating device. In this way, you can dial in the proper temperature for the habitat.

The drawback to rheostats is that they only regulate the amount of power going to the device – they do not monitor the cage temperature or adjust the power flow automatically. In practice, even with the same level of power entering the device, the amount of heat generated by most heat sources varies over the course of the day.

If you set the rheostat so that it keeps the cage at the right temperature in the morning, it may become too hot by the middle of the day. Conversely, setting the proper temperature during the middle of the day may leave the morning temperatures too cool.

Care must be taken to ensure that the rheostat controller is not inadvertently bumped or jostled, causing the temperature to rise or fall outside of healthy parameters.

Thermostats

Thermostats are similar to rheostats, except that they also feature a temperature probe that monitors the temperature in the cage (or under the basking source). This allows the thermostat to adjust the power going to the device as necessary to maintain a predetermined temperature.

For example, if you place the temperature probe under a basking spot powered by a radiant heat panel, the thermostat will keep the temperature relatively constant under the basking site.

There are two different types of thermostats:

On-Off Thermostats

"On-Off" thermostats work by cutting the power to the device when the probe's temperature reaches a given temperature.

For example, if the thermostat were set to 85 degrees Fahrenheit (29 degrees Celsius), the heating device would turn off whenever the temperature exceeds this threshold. When the temperature falls below 85, the thermostat restores power to the unit, and the heater begins functioning again. This cycle will continue to repeat, thus maintaining the temperature within a relatively small range.

Be aware that on-off thermostats have a "lag" factor, meaning that they do not turn off when the temperature reaches a given temperature. They turn off when the temperature is a few degrees *above* that temperature, and then turn back on when the temperate is a little *below* the set point. Because of this, it is important to avoid setting the temperature at the limits of your pet's acceptable range. Some premium models have an adjustable amount of threshold for this factor, which is helpful.

Pulse Proportional Thermostats

Pulse proportional thermostats work by constantly sending pulses of electricity to the heater. By varying the rate of pulses, the amount of energy reaching the heating devices varies.

A small computer inside the thermostat adjusts this rate to match the set-point temperature as measured by the probe. Accordingly, pulse proportional thermostats maintain much more consistent temperatures than on-off thermostats do.

Lights should not be used with thermostats, as the constant flickering may stress your snake. Conversely, heat pads, heat tape, radiant heat panels and ceramic heat emitters should always be used with either a rheostat or, preferably, a thermostat to avoid overheating your snake.

Thermostat Failure

If used for long enough, all thermostats eventually fail. The question is will yours fail today or twenty years from now. While some thermostats fail in the "off" position, a thermostat that fails in the "on" position may overheat your snakes. Unfortunately, tales of entire collections being lost to a faulty thermostat are too common.

Accordingly, it behooves the keeper to acquire high-quality thermostats. Some keepers use two thermostats, connected in series arrangement. By setting the second thermostat (the "backup thermostat") a few degrees higher than the setting used on the "primary thermostat," you safeguard yourself against the failure of either unit.

In such a scenario, the backup thermostat allows the full power coming to it to travel through to the heating device, as the temperature never reaches its higher set-point temperature.

However, if the first unit fails in the "on" position, the second thermostat will keep the temperatures from rising too high. The temperature will rise a few degrees in accordance with the higher set-point temperature, but it will not get hot enough to harm your snakes.

If the backup thermostat fails in the "on" position, the first thermostat retains control. If either fails in the "off" position, the temperature will fall until you rectify the situation, but a brief exposure to relatively cool temperatures is unlikely to be fatal.

Nighttime Heating

In most circumstances, you should provide your water snake with a minor temperature drop at night. If the enclosure temperatures remain above about 65 degrees Fahrenheit (18 degrees Celsius) – about 70 degrees Fahrenheit (21 degrees Celsius) for young individuals – you will not need to use a heat source at night. Instead, you can simply switch your heating device off at night, and turn it back on in the morning.

You can also plug the heating devices (and thermostats or rheostats) into a lamp-timer to automate the process. Some thermostats even have features that adjust the temperature of the thermostat during the night, lowering it to a specified level.

Those who must provide some type of nocturnal heat source can do so in a number of ways. Virtually any non-light-emitting heat source will function adequately in this capacity. Ceramic heating elements, radiant heat panels and heat pads, cables and tape all work well for supplying nocturnal heat.

Red lights can be used in reflector domes to provide heat as well. In fact, red lights can be used for heating during the day and night, but the cage will not be illuminated very well, unless other lights are incorporated during the day.

Incorporating Thermal Mass

One underutilized technique that is helpful for raising the temperature of a cage is to increase the cage's thermal mass.

Rocks, large water dishes and ceramic cage decorations are examples of items that may work in such contexts. These objects will absorb heat from the heat source, and then re-radiate heat into the habitat.

Adding thermal mass to a habitat changes the thermal characteristics greatly. By simply adding a large rock, the cage may eventually warm up a few degrees.

Raising the cage's thermal mass also helps to reduce the cage's rate of cooling in the evening. By placing a thick rock under the basking light, it will absorb heat all day and radiate this heat after the lights turn off. Eventually it will reach room temperature, but this may take hours.

Always remember to monitor the cage surface temperatures and ambient temperatures regularly after changing the thermal characteristics of the cage. Pay special attention to the surface temperatures of items placed on or under a heat source.

Experiment with different amounts of thermal mass in the cage. Use items of different sizes, shapes and materials, and see how the cage temperatures change. In general, the more thermal mass in the cage, the more constant the temperature will stay.

Chapter 8: Lighting the Enclosure

Assuming they are provided with appropriate temperatures, most water snakes can likely survive with little more than the incidental light entering the cage.

However, while supplemental lighting is not a necessary component of water snake maintenance, high quality lighting will help showcase your pet's incredible colors and iridescence. It may also encourage your pet to exhibit natural behaviors and feed better, although this has not been conclusively demonstrated.

Because additional lighting may raise the cage temperatures, it is important to monitor the cage temperatures after adding or changing the type of light sources used. While fluorescent lights and small LEDs do not produce a lot of heat, they may generate enough to warm small cages to undesirable levels.

Lighting Options

A number of lighting options are available for interested keepers. While all of these options will make the cage brighter and accentuate your pet's coloration, some accomplish this goal better than others do.

Lights that produce a balanced spectrum with a high color-rendering index will make your snake look his best, but even economy bulbs will allow you to see your animal better.

Reptile-specific lights are not required, as water snakes do not appear to require exposure to ultraviolet radiation to metabolize their dietary calcium and vitamin D, as many lizards and turtles do.

Heat Lamp Bulbs

In addition to warmth, heat lamps provide some supplemental illumination for the enclosure. However, as their primary purpose is to heat – not illuminate -- the enclosure, most bulbs used in heat lamps produce relatively poor light.

Wattage, price point and other factors drive product development and consumer choice – not light quality. Most incandescent bulbs produce very yellow, unbalanced light. Nevertheless, some manufacturers make incandescent bulbs that produce a relatively balanced spectrum, with respectable CRI.

Fluorescent Lights
Fluorescent bulbs are the best option for supplemental lighting. These lights produce higher quality light than incandescent bulbs do, and they do not produce very much heat.

You can use either linear fluorescent lights or "compact" fluorescent bulbs. Compact fluorescent bulbs can be used in reflector domes instead of incandescent bulbs while linear fluorescent lights require special ballasts.

LED Lights
Recently, LED technology has become much more affordable, and some keepers have begun using LED lights to brighten their enclosures.

The quality of light produced by LEDs offer surpasses that produced by any other lights, so these bulbs make a great choice, provided that their cost is not prohibitive.

Photoperiod
Provide your water snake with a consistent day-night cycle to avoid causing him stress. Use a lamp timer to help keep the light cycle consistent, and make it unnecessary for you to do so manually.

Most water snakes receive between 12 and 14 hours of daylight during the summer, but only about 10 to 12 hours of daylight during the winter. This obviously varies based on their geographic origin; those inhabiting the northern United States or southern Canada enjoy fewer hours of sunlight in any season, than their counterparts living in Florida do.

For basic pet maintenance purposes, it is acceptable to provide your pet with a 12-hour photoperiod throughout the year. But breeding attempts may be bolstered by the adoption of a fluctuating photoperiod, ranging from about 10 hours of light in the winter to 14 hours of light in the summer.

Chapter 9: Substrate and Furniture

Once you have purchased or constructed your water snake's enclosure, you must place appropriate items inside it. In general, these items take the form of an appropriate substrate and the proper cage furniture.

Acceptable Substrates

Substrates are used to give your snake a comfortable surface on which to crawl and to absorb any liquids present.

There are a variety of acceptable choices, all of which have different benefits and drawbacks.

Paper Products

The easiest and safest substrates for water snakes are paper products in sheet form. While regular newspaper is the most common choice, paper towels, unprinted newspaper, butcher's paper or commercially produced cage liners are equally acceptable.

Paper substrates are very easy to maintain, but they do not last very long and must be completely replaced when they are soiled. Accordingly, they must be changed regularly -- at least once per week.

Use several layers of paper products to provide sufficient absorbency and a little bit of cushion for your snake.

Paper Pulp Products

Many commercial pulp products have become available over the last decade. Comprised of recycled wood fibers, these products are very absorbent, but they may rot quickly when exposed to moisture, so they are not ideal for water snake maintenance.

Cypress Mulch

Cypress mulch is a popular substrate choice for many species, including water snakes. The mulch looks attractive and holds humidity well.

Cypress mulch is available from most home improvement and garden centers, as well as pet supply retailers. No matter the source you use, be sure that the product contains 100 percent cypress mulch without any demolition or salvage content.

Fir (Orchid) Bark
Fir bark (sometimes called orchid bark) is an attractive substrate that absorbs and releases water effectively, making it well suited for water snake maintenance.

The primary drawback to fir bark is its high cost.

Soils
While not commonly used by commercial water snake breeders or many hobbyists, soil is an acceptable substrate. You can dig up your own soil, purchase organic soil products or mix your own blend.

Avoid products containing perlite, manure, fertilizers, pre-emergent herbicides or other additives. Sterilizing the soil before adding it to the enclosure is not strictly necessary, but it is probably wise to do so.

Substrate Comparison Chart

Substrate	Pros	Cons
Newspaper	Safe, free, easiest substrate for keeping the cage clean.	May be unattractive to some. Purchase pre-printed paper if you are uncomfortable with the ink. Cannot be spot-cleaned.
Paper Towels	Safe, highly absorbent.	May be unattractive to some. Cannot be spot-cleaned.
Commercial Paper Product	Safe and easy to maintain.	May be unattractive to some. Can be expensive with long term use. Cannot be spot-cleaned.
Cypress Mulch	Allows snake to burrow, easy to spot-clean. Many find it attractive. Retains moisture well.	May be ingested, sharp sticks may harm snakes, messy, can be expensive.
Fir (Orchid) Bark	Allows snake to burrow, easy to spot-clean. Many find it attractive. Retains moisture well.	May be ingested, messy, can be expensive.
Pulp Paper Products	Allows snake to burrow, easy to spot-clean.	May be unattractive to some. May be ingested, messy, can be expensive.

Substrates to Avoid

Some substrates are completely inappropriate for water snake maintenance, and should be avoided. These include:

Aspen and Pine Shavings -- While popular, these types of wood shavings rot quickly when wet, they do not make a good choice for water snakes.

Cedar Shavings – Cedar shavings produce toxic fumes that may sicken or kill your snake. Always avoid cedar shavings.

Sand – Sand is too dusty for water snakes and poorly suited for use in high-humidity habitats. It may also cause algae blooms to occur in water reservoirs.

Gravel – You can use large gravel as a substrate, but its problems outweigh its benefits. Gravel must be washed when soiled, which is laborious and time consuming. Gravel is also quite heavy, which can cause headaches for the keeper.

Artificial Turf – Artificial turf is a poor substrate for most snakes, including water snakes.

Cage Furniture

In addition to a water reservoir and substrate, you must provide your snake with hiding opportunities to keep him feeling secure. Hiding places are critical for your snake's well-being and are in no way optional.

In addition to hiding spots, you can also add plants and climbing perches to the habitat. These are not at all mandatory, but they may provide your snake with a higher quality of life.

Hiding Spots

You can use a variety of items to create your snake's hiding spot, from commercially produced, decorative items to a crumpled piece of newspaper.

To a large extent, you can let your own preferences guide your choice. You simply need to ensure the hiding spots you offer are safe, are either easy to clean or cheap enough to replace regularly, and fit the snake snuggly.

Ideally, you should provide at least one hiding spot on the warm side of the cage, and one hiding spot on the cool side of the cage.

Commercial Hide Boxes
Commercial hide boxes come in a wide variety of shapes, sizes and styles. Opt for those constructed from non-porous materials (ceramic or plastic) and designed to fit your snake snuggly.

Plastic Storage Boxes
While not that attractive, small, opaque storage boxes make functional hiding places. Simply discard the lid to the container, flip the tub upside down and cut an entrance hole in the side.

Plant Saucers
The saucers designed to collect the water that overfills potted plants make excellent hiding locations. Just as with a plastic storage box, you simply need to flip a plant saucer upside down and cut a small opening in the side for a door. Clay or plastic saucers can be used, but clay saucers are hard to cut. If you punch an entrance hole into a clay saucer, you must sand or grind down the edges to prevent hurting your snake.

Plates
Plastic, paper or ceramic plates make good hiding locations for small water snakes in cages that use particulate substrates. This will allow the snake to burrow up under the plate through the substrate, and hide in a very tight space. Such hiding places also make it very easy to access your snake while he is hiding.

Cardboard Boxes
While you must discard and replace them anytime they become soiled, small cardboard boxes can make suitable hide boxes. Be sure to select one of the proper size, to ensure your snake feels safe while he is inside.

Commercial "Half-Logs"
Many pet stores sell U-shaped pieces of wood that resemble half of a hollow log. While these are sometimes attractive looking items, they are not appropriate hide spots when used as intended. The U-shaped construction means that the snake will not feel the top of the hide when he is laying inside. These hides can be functional if they are partially buried, thus reducing the height of the hide.

Cork Bark

Real bark cut from the Cork Oak (*Quercus suber*), "cork bark" is a wonderful looking decorative item that can be implemented in a variety of ways. Usually cork bark is available in tube shape or in flat sheets. Flat pieces are better for smaller water snakes, although exceptionally large snakes may be able to use tubular sections adequately. Flat pieces should only be used with particulate, rather than sheet-like substrates so that the snake can get under them easily.

Cork bark may be slightly difficult to clean, as its surface contains numerous indentations and crevices. Use hot water, soap and a sturdy brush to clean the pieces.

Paper Towel Tubes

Small sections of paper towel tubes make suitable hiding spots for small water snakes, although the snakes quickly become too large for such hides. They do not last very long, so they require frequent replacement. They often work best if flattened slightly.

Newspaper or Paper Towels

Several sheets of newspaper or paper towels placed on top of the substrate (whether sheet-like or particulate) make suitable hiding spots. Many professional breeders use paper-hiding spaces because it is such a simple and economically feasible solution. Some keepers crumple a few of the sheets to give the stack of paper more height.

Unusual Items

Some keepers like to express their individuality by using unique or unusual items as hiding spots. Some have used handmade ceramic items, while others have used skulls or turtle shells. If the four primary criteria previously discussed are met, there is no reason such items will not make suitable hiding spaces.

Humid Hides

In addition to security, snakes also derive another benefit from many of their hiding spaces in the wild. Most hiding places feature higher humidity than the surrounding air.

By spending a lot of time in such places, snakes are able to avoid dehydration in habitats where water is scarce. Additionally, time spent in these humid retreats aids in the shedding process. You should take steps to provide similar opportunities in captivity.

Humid hides can be made by placing damp sphagnum moss in a plastic container. The moss should not be saturated, but merely damp. You can also use damp paper towels or newspaper to increase the humidity of a hide box.

Some keepers prefer to keep humid hides in the habitat at all times, while others use them periodically – usually preceding shed cycles. Humid hides should never be the only hides available to the snake. Always use them in addition to dry hides.

Plants

While not necessities for sound husbandry, both live and artificial plants provide additional visual barriers for your snake and help to increase the complexity of the cage. They can also increase the aesthetic appeal of the habitat.

Artificial plants are simpler to select, install and maintain than live plants are, but live plants help to maintain good air quality and raise the humidity of the habitat.

Artificial plants require relatively little effort to install. Simply rinse them off and add them to the cage in a visually pleasing manner. Live plants, on the other hand, are often coated with pesticides or plagued by insects, so more effort is required before placing them in the habitat.

Always wash live plants before placing them in the enclosure to help remove any pesticide residues. It is also wise to discard the potting soil used for the plant and replace it with fresh soil, which you know contains no pesticides, perlite or fertilizer.

While you can plant cage plants directly in soil substrates, this complicates maintenance and makes it difficult to replace the substrate regularly. Accordingly, it is generally preferable to keep the plant in some type of container. Be sure to use a catch tray under the pot, so that water draining from the container does not flow into the cage.

You must use care to select a species that will thrive in your snake's enclosure. For example, plants that require direct sunlight will perish in the relatively dim light of the cage.

Instead, you must choose plants that will thrive in shaded conditions. Similarly, because you will be misting the cage regularly, and trying to keep the internal environment as humid as possible, few succulents or other plants adapted to arid habitats will live in a water snake enclosure.

Some of the most common choices that are likely safe and well suited for your water snake's enclosures include:

-Devil's Ivy (*Pothos* spp.)

-Small fig trees (*Ficus* spp.)

-Small umbrella trees (*Schefflera arboricola*)

-Split-leaf philodendrons (*Monstera deliciosa*)

-Assorted ferns (especially *Pteridophytas spp.)*

-Peace lilies (*Spathiphyllum* spp.)

-Pawpaws (*Asimina* spp.)

-*Neoregelia* bromeliads

-*Aechmea* bromeliads

Perches
Water snakes are primarily terrestrial snakes that do not require perches in captivity. However, many individuals will climb if provided with the opportunity to do so, and some keepers provide these types of opportunities to their snakes.

You can purchase climbing branches from pet and craft stores, or you can collect them yourself. When collecting your own branches, try to use branches that are still attached to trees (make sure you always obtain permission before removing them). Such branches will harbor fewer insects and other invertebrate pests than dead branches will.

Many different types of branches can be used in water snake cages. Most non-aromatic hardwoods suffice.

Always wash branches with plenty of hot water and a stiff, metal-bristled scrub brush to remove as much dirt, dust and fungus as possible before placing them in your snake's cage. Clean stubborn spots with a little bit of dish soap, but be sure to rinse them thoroughly afterwards.

It is also advisable to sterilize branches before placing them in a cage. The easiest way to do so is by placing the branch in a 300-degree oven for about 15 minutes. Doing so should kill the vast majority of pests and pathogens lurking inside the wood.

Some keepers like to cover their branches with a water-sealing product. This is acceptable if a non-toxic product is used and the branches are allowed to air dry for several days before being placed in the cage. However, as branches are relatively easy to replace, it is not necessary to seal them if you plan to replace them.

You can often place branches diagonally across the enclosure, in such a way that alleviates the need for direct attachment to the cage. However, horizontal branches will require secure points of attachment so they do not fall and injure your pet.

You can attach the branches to the cage in a variety of different ways. Be sure to make it easy to remove the branches as necessary, so you can clean them easily.

You can use hooks and eye-screws to suspend branches, which allows for quick and easy removal, but it is only applicable for cages with walls that will accept and support the eye-screws. You can also make "closet rod holders" by cutting a slot into small PVC caps, which are attached to the cage frame.

Chapter 10: Maintaining the Captive Habitat

Now that you have acquired your water snake and set up the enclosure, you must develop a protocol for maintaining his habitat. While snake habitats require major maintenance every month or so, they only require minor daily maintenance.

In addition to designing a husbandry protocol, you must embrace a record-keeping system to track your snake's growth and health.

Cleaning and Maintenance Procedures

Once you have decided on the proper enclosure for your pet, you must keep your snake fed, hydrated and ensure that the habitat stays in proper working order to keep your captive healthy and comfortable.

Some tasks must be completed each day, while others are should be performed weekly, monthly or annually.

Daily

- Monitor the ambient and surface temperatures of the habitat.

- Provide drinking water by misting the cage

- Spot clean the cage to remove any feces, urates or pieces of shed skin

- Ensure that the lights, latches and other moving parts are in working order

- Verify that your snake is acting normally and appears healthy. You do not necessarily need to handle him to do so

- Ensure that the humidity and ventilation are at appropriate levels.

Weekly

- Change sheet-like substrates (newspaper, paper towels, etc.).

- Feed your snake as appropriate (some keepers feed more than once per week)

- Clean the inside surfaces of the enclosure.

- Inspect your snake closely for any signs of injury, parasites or illness

- Wash and sterilize all food dishes.

Monthly
- Break down the cage completely, remove and discard particulate substrates.

- Sterilize drip containers and similar equipment in a mild bleach solution.

- Measure and weigh your snake.

- Photograph your pet (recommended, but not imperative).

- Prune any plants as necessary.

Annually
- Replace the batteries in your thermometers and any other devices that use them.

Cleaning your snake's cage and furniture is relatively simple. Regardless of the way it became soiled, the basic process remains the same:

1. Rinse the object

2. Using a scrub brush or sponge and soapy water, remove any organic debris from the object.

3. Rinse the object thoroughly.

4. Disinfect the object.

5. Re-rinse the object.

6. Dry the object.

Chemicals & Tools
A variety of chemicals and tools are necessary for reptile care. Save yourself some time by purchasing dedicated cleaning products and keeping them in the same place that you keep your tools.

Spray Bottles

Misting your snake and his habitat with fresh water is one of the best ways to increase the cage humidity. You can do this with a small, handheld misting bottle or a larger, pressurized unit (such as those used to spray herbicides). Automated units are available, but they are rarely cost-effective unless you are caring for a large colony of snakes.

Scrub Brushes or Sponges

It helps to have a few different types of scrub brushes and sponges on hand for scrubbing and cleaning different items. Use the least abrasive sponge or brush suitable for the task to prevent wearing out cage items prematurely. Do not use abrasive materials on glass or acrylic surfaces. Steel-bristled brushes work well for scrubbing coarse, wooden items, such as branches.

Spatulas and Putty Knives

Spatulas, putty knives and similar tools are often helpful for cleaning reptile cages. For example, urates (which are not soluble in anything short of hot lava) often become stuck on cage walls or furniture. Instead of trying to dissolve them with harsh chemicals, just scrape them away with a sturdy plastic putty knife.

Spatulas and putty knives can also be helpful for removing wet newspaper, which often becomes stuck to the floor of the cage.

Small Vacuums

Small, handheld vacuums are very helpful for sucking up the dust left behind from substrates. They are also helpful for cleaning the cracks and crevices around the cage doors. A shop vacuum, with suitable hoses and attachments, can also be helpful, if you have enough room to store it.

Steam Cleaners

Steam cleaners are very effective for sterilizing cages, water bowls and durable cage props after they have been cleaned. In fact, steam is often a better choice than chemical disinfectants, as it will not leave behind a toxic residue. Never use a steam cleaner near your snake, the plants in his cage or any other living organisms.

Soap

Use a gentle, non-scented dish soap. Antibacterial soap is preferred, but not necessary. Most people use far more soap than is necessary -- a few drops mixed with a quantity of water is usually sufficient to help remove surface pollutants.

Bleach

Bleach (diluted to one-half cup per gallon of water) makes an excellent disinfectant. Be careful not to spill any on clothing, carpets or furniture, as it is likely to discolor the objects.

Always be sure to rinse objects thoroughly after using bleach and be sure that you cannot detect any residual odor. Bleach does not work as a disinfectant when in contact with organic substances; accordingly, items must be cleaned before you can disinfect them.

Veterinarian Approved Disinfectant

Many commercial products are available that are designed to be safe for their pets. Consult with your veterinarian about the best product for your situation, its method of use and its proper dilution.

Avoid Phenols

Always avoid cleaners that contain phenols, as they are extremely toxic to some reptiles. In general, do not use household cleaning products to avoid exposing your pet to toxic chemicals.

Keeping Records

It is important to keep records regarding your pet's health, growth and feeding, as well as any other important details. In the past, reptile keepers would do so on small index cards or in a notebook. In the modern world, technological solutions may be easier. For example, you can use your computer or mobile device to keep track of the pertinent info about your pet.

You can record as much information about your pet as you like, and the more information to you record, the better. But minimally, you should record the following:

Pedigree and Origin Information

Be sure to record the source of your snake, the date on which you acquired him and any other data that is available. Breeders will often provide customers with information regarding the sire, dam, date of birth, weights and feeding records, but other sources will rarely offer comparable data.

Feeding Information
Record the date of each feeding, as well as the type of food item(s) offered. It is also helpful to record any preferences you may observe or any meals that are refused.

Weights and Length
Because you look at your pet frequently, it is difficult to appreciate how quickly he is (or isn't) growing. Accordingly, it is important to track his size diligently.

Weigh your snake with a high quality digital scale. The scale must be sensitive to one-tenth-gram increments to be useful for very small individuals.

It is often easiest to use a dedicated "weighing container" with a known weight to measure your snake. This way, you will not have to keep the lizard stationary on the scale's platform – you can simply place him in the container and place the entire container on the scale. Subtract the weight of the container to obtain the weight of your pet.

You can measure your snake's length as well, but it is not as important as tracking his weight.

Maintenance Information
Record all of the noteworthy events associated with your pet's care. While it is not necessary to note that you misted the cage each day, it is appropriate to record the dates on which you changed the substrate or sterilized the cage.

Whenever you purchase new equipment, supplies or caging, note the date and source. This not only helps to remind you when you purchased the items, but it may help you track down a source for the items in the future, if necessary.

Breeding Information
If you intend to breed your snake, you should record all details associated with pre-breeding conditioning, cycling, introductions, matings, color changes, copulations and parturition.

Record all pertinent information about any resulting litters as well, including the number of young and unfertilized ova.

Record Keeping Samples
The following are two different examples of suitable recording systems.

The first example demonstrates a simple approach that is employed by many with small collections: keeping notes on paper. It does not matter *how* you keep records, just that you *do* keep records.

The second example is reminiscent of the style employed by many with large collections. Because such keepers often have numerous animals, the notes are very simple, and require a minimum amount of writing or typing.

Date	Notes
6-25-13	*Acquired "Swamp Thing" the northern water snake from a breeder named Mark at the in-town reptile expo. Mark explained that Swamp Thing's scientific name is Nerodia sipedon sipedon. Cost was $50. Mark said that Swamp Thing is a boy. Mark said he purchased him in March, but he does not know the exact date.*
6-26-13	*Swamp Thing spent the night in the container I bought him in. I purchased a small aquarium and heat lamp at the pet store. I bought the thermometer at the hardware store next door and ordered a non-contact thermometer online. I added a large branch I found outside so he can climb.*
6-27-13	*Swamp Thing spent the day exploring his cage. He isn't using the branch yet, but he seems comfortable.*
6-29-13	*I fed Swamp Thing 10 guppies today. He still looked kinda hungry, but I think that was enough for the day.*
7-5-13	*I fed Swamp Thing three more guppies today. I've got to get some more from the pet store before next feeding.*
7-8-13	*Swamp Thing's eyes turned bright blue today, so I think that means he is going to shed soon. I'm excited to see how bright his colors will look once he's done.*

ID Number:	44522	Genus: Species/Sub:	Nerodia Sipedon	Gender: DOB:	Male 3/20/15	CARD #2
6.30.15 6 Guppies	7.03.15 Blue	7.14.15 6 Guppies	7.25.15 7 Guppies	8.10.15 Blue		
7.01.15 3 Guppies	7.10.15 Shed	7.18.15 Full Cage Clean	7.30.15 2 Tadpoles	8.19.15 Shed		
7.02.15 Cleaned water filter	7.11.15 8 Guppies	7.19.15 8 Guppies	8.01.15 3 Guppies	8.20.15 Full Cage Clean		

A plainbelly water snake.

71

Chapter 11: Feeding Your Water Snake

For new keepers, few aspects of water snake care are as exciting as feeding their pet. However, water snakes often present a few challenges that other common pet snakes do not.

Nevertheless, with the appropriate effort, ingenuity and patience, most keepers are able to get their water snake eating regularly.

Prey Species

There are a few different prey species that you can feed to your water snake. Often, it will be necessary to experiment with several different species before discovering which one your snake prefers.

Most water snakes will readily eat live fish. Goldfish are often used in this capacity, but goldfish frequently harbor significant parasite loads, thanks to the way they are typically farmed. Guppies and other small species are acceptable, as are shiners and fathead minnows.

You can also feed your snake fresh, pre-killed, whole fish, such as you may find in some farmer's markets or grocery stores. The problem here is finding fish that are small enough; however, you can ask the staff, who may be able to provide you with fish that were deemed too small. Do not feed your snake frozen or canned fish.

Other keepers prefer to feed their water snake frogs. Because most frogs sold in the country are wild-caught, parasites can be a concern for them as well. However, with proper cage hygiene and appropriate veterinary care, this is unlikely to cause a big problem.

Avoid feeding your snake frogs that may produce harmful toxins, such as toads, gray tree frogs, Cuban tree frogs or (obviously) poison dart frogs. Instead, stick to frogs of the genus *Rana*. This includes bullfrogs, pig frogs and green frogs. You can also try to feed your water snake the tadpoles produced by these species.

The other primary option – and the preferred one, from the keeper's point of view – is commercially reared rodents. Many water snake species will consume the odd rodent in the wild, and they are usually capable of doing so in captivity as well.

However, it is rarely easy to coax a water snake into eating a rodent, so you'll often need to cover it in the slime from a frog or fish to make it smell like more typical prey. Never offer a fully furred, live rodent to a snake, as it may bite your snake and cause serious – potentially fatal – wounds.

Prey Size

Regardless of the prey you intend to offer your water snake, you must be sure that the prey is the appropriate size. Foods that are too small may not appeal to the snake, while those that are too big can cause injuries to your snake.

Most water snakes want prey that is at least the size of their head, but not more than about 1.25 times their midbody diameter. Some water snakes occasionally consume frogs or fish larger than this, but these are slimy animals, which will slide down their throat quite easily.

Usually one properly sized frog per meal is easy to obtain, but you'll usually be purchasing feeder fish that are relatively small. Accordingly, keepers usually provide their water snake with 5 to 12 small fish per feeding.

If you feed rodents to your water snake, it is wise to err on the side of caution. Try to feed your snake rodents that are about the same size as your snake's midbody diameter.

It is always better to feed your snake items that are too small, rather than too large. Additionally, water snakes tend to eat slightly more frequently than some other snakes do, so smaller items simply make more sense.

How to Offer Food

Unlike rodents, which can and do fight back when pursued by snakes, small frogs and fish are unlikely to harm a snake who is attempting to consume it. Accordingly, it is not necessary to offer pre-killed prey. Additionally, water snakes frequently respond best to live prey.

If you are feeding your water snake frogs, you can simply release them into the enclosure. It is often most effective to do so in the late

73

afternoon or early evening, although you can feed at any time of the day.

If you are feeding your snake fish, you'll need to have a large water reservoir (which most water snake habitats should have, anyway). This can be the water bowl or some type of permanent "pool." Simply release the fish into the container and your snake will catch and consume them.

You'll need to clean and re-fill the water reservoir after every feeding, or use very high-quality filtration units, if you maintain a permanent reservoir, as fish foul water very quickly.

If you do feed your water snake rodents, only offer pre-killed (or frozen-thawed) rodents via tongs. You may have to move the rodent about to help catch the snake's attention and make it look alive.

Feeding Frequency

Most snake keepers provide food once per week. Assuming the food provided is the correct size, and you provide enough calories over time, this works well for boas, pythons, kingsnakes and rat snakes.

However, water snakes often benefit from slightly more frequent meals, as their prey often digests very quickly. Accordingly, it is often best to feed water snakes once every 4 to 6 days.

Snakes will refuse food from time to time, and this is rarely cause for concern. Simply discard the food item and offer food again at the next scheduled feeding. However, if your snake refuses food for a month or longer, contact your veterinarian.

Because feeder-sized fish and frogs are rarely dangerous to snakes, it is also possible to feed them on an ad libitum basis. This means maintaining a few frogs or a school of fish in the snake's habitat on a more-or-less constant basis. As you notice the feeder population declining, you replace those that were lost.

This introduces an entirely new level of complexity to the habitat (you'll have to feed the feeders, for starters), and will require you to make several adjustments to your husbandry procedures. Accordingly, this is not a good strategy for novices, although it can work well in professionally maintained displays.

Avoiding Regurgitation

Just like humans, snakes may regurgitate or vomit food items in response to a variety of stimuli, including toxins, stress and temperature extremes.

Accordingly, it is important to feed your snake the highest quality foods possible, avoid causing the animal stress (especially right after meals) and maintaining the habitat within the correct temperature range.

Vomiting and regurgitation not only saddle the keeper with unpleasant clean up duties, they are very hard on the snake's body. Among other problems, vomiting can lead to dehydration and additional stress.

Give snakes that vomit at least one full week before offering food again. One of the biggest mistakes keepers make when dealing with a snake that has regurgitated is that they try to make up for the lost meal too quickly. This stresses the snake's digestive system and can lead to long-term, chronic problems

Chapter 12: Water

Like most other animals, water snakes require drinking water to remain healthy. However, they also spend a lot of time foraging and soaking in the water, so most keepers prefer to provide them with a large water reservoir.

While it is not absolutely imperative that you provide them with a bowl or dish large enough to accommodate their bodies, it will help provide them with a higher quality of life and encourage natural behaviors.

Put another way, if you don't want to go to the trouble of providing a large water container for your snake, you should probably consider opting for a snake that inhabits drier habitats.

Water Reservoir

You can use a variety of containers for your snake's water dish. Commercially produced water dishes are one of the better choices, although virtually any smooth-sided, non-toxic container will work.

If you do not intend to allow your snake to enter the water, a 4- to 6-inch-diameter dish will work. If you want to give your snake room to soak and swim, you can make it as large as you like.

Be sure to check the water dish daily and ensure that the water is clean. Empty, wash and refill the water dish any time it becomes contaminated with substrate, shed skin, urates or feces.

Some keepers prefer to use dechlorinated or bottled water for their snakes; however, untreated tap water is used by many keepers with no ill effects.

Filtration

If you intend on using a very large, permanent water reservoir in the habitat (akin to a small "pond"), you'll need to use an aquarium filter to ensure the water stays clean.

Always use a filter rated for at least twice the amount of water you are trying to keep clean, as water snakes (and any food items you place in the water reservoir) will foul the water very quickly.

Even when using a filter, you'll need to conduct a partial water change each week. To do so, simply remove about half of the water in the reservoir and replace it with a similar quantity of clean water.

Chapter 13: Interacting with Your Water Snake

Many keepers enjoy handling pet snakes; assuming that they do not occur too frequently, gentle, brief handling sessions are unlikely to stress your pet. In fact, it is necessary to handle your snake from time to time – not only so that you can move him while you clean his cage, but also to monitor his health.

Unfortunately, many water snakes react poorly to their keeper's advances. However, every water snake is an individual; some captive raised water snakes eventually learn to tolerate gentle handling, but most remain defensive throughout their lives.

No matter what side of the spectrum your snake falls on, you must be able to handle your pet when necessary – even if he is very defensive.

Picking Up a Water Snake

Try to move with a purpose once you open the cage door. Don't stare at your snake for 15 minutes as you try to work up your nerve. This often makes snakes feel insecure, which leads to defensive behaviors.

Pick up your water snake by gently sliding your fingers underneath his body and lifting him into the air. Small snakes can be supported adequately with one hand, but two hands are necessary for lifting medium or large specimens.

Young water snakes are usually nippy, but many calm down over time with frequent interaction. The bites of young water snakes are harmless (many will not even break the skin of your fingers), but they still make many beginning keepers nervous.

If you would like to avoid the bites and strikes of small water snakes, you can cover the snake with a paper towel before picking him up. This usually keeps the snake calmer and discourages them from biting.

Alternatively, you can use a snake hook (or an improvised version thereof) to lift your snake from the ground. Be careful not to keep the snake on the hook for an extended length of time, as the hook may put pressure on the animal's bones or internal organs. Instead, strive to quickly slip the hook under the snake near mid-body, lift the snake up and transfer him to the intended location.

If necessary, you can rely almost entirely on a snake hook for moving your snake around. You can simply lift him out of his cage, place him in a temporary cage while you clean his habitat, and then (using the hook), repeat the process in reverse. This means that you needn't come into direct contact with an aggressive water snake during the course of routine maintenance (you will still need to handle your snake to inspect his health).

No matter how aggressive the snake is, you should avoid "pinning" him behind the head, as some keepers do with venomous species. Inexperienced keepers often apply too much pressure to the snake's neck, which can have tragic consequences.

Gloves provide another alternative for those who desire some protection while handling their water snake. Virtually any type of thick glove will work (batting gloves, work gloves, welding gloves, etc.), as the teeth of young water snakes are not very long.

Gloves only provide a small amount of protection against larger specimens. While the longer teeth of adults may allow them to penetrate gloves that young specimens cannot, adults are also able to strike a lot farther than small specimens can. Large individuals can strike far enough to reach your arms, torso or face, while the snake is in your hands.

Holding a Water Snake

Now that you have picked up your water snake, you must hold him in a way that prevents stress or injury.

The best way to hold a snake and keep it from feeling threatened is to provide it with plenty of support and allow it to crawl freely through your hands. Avoid restraining your snake or gripping it tightly with your hands, as this will cause it to feel like prey. Instead, simply support its body weight, and allow it to crawl from one hand to the other.

It is always wise to handle the snake over a table or other object to prevent his from falling to the floor, should he make a sudden move.

Always be patient and gentle when transferring your water snake to or from your hands. Never attempt to pry your pet from a perch or pull him by his tail. Instead, you can simply tickle his tail, which will usually cause him to release his grip and move forward.

Handling Your Snake Safely

Even tame water snakes must be handled safely. While they are unlikely to cause grave bodily harm, large specimens can certainly inflict a nasty bite. Accordingly, you must avoid placing the snake near your face (or anyone else's face).

Always be sure to avoid smelling like potential prey when handling water snakes, and refrain from handling snakes in the presence of unsupervised children or pets.

Handling Your Snake Responsibly

Always realize that you are responsible for your snake while you are holding it. Accidents can and do happen. Such occurrences are very bad for snakes, snake keepers and the entire snake-keeping hobby, and must be avoided.

Essentially, this means that you must keep your snake far enough away from other people that he cannot bite them, should he become frightened or startled. It is also worth mentioning that scared snakes may defecate or release urates – sometimes in a semi-projectile fashion.

Never handle your snake in a public situation. Do not take your snake to the park or to the local fast food restaurant. Your snake is not a toy, he does not appreciate "hanging out" in this manner, and it makes snake keepers everywhere look bad.

Snakes frighten many people and you should always be sensitive to this fact. Rather than playing into these fears, seek to educate people about snakes rather than shock them by bringing them to inappropriate events and locations.

In the Event of a Bite

If your water snake bites you, remain calm. If it is a defensive bite, the snake will usually release its hold on your skin quickly. If this occurs, you can simply close the cage or return the snake to his enclosure.

After returning the snake to his cage, wash the wound thoroughly with soap and warm water. Consult your doctor if the bite is serious, if it will not stop bleeding or if you can feel teeth lodged in the wound.

If the snake does not release his grip (such as occurs in a feeding bite), the best thing to do is place him in a bucket of cold water. Most snakes will voluntarily let go after being submerged for a minute or two. As with a defensive bite, you should wash the wound, and contact your doctor if the wound is serious.

Transporting Your Pet

Although you should strive to avoid any unnecessary travel with your snake, circumstances (such as illness) often demand that you do.

Strive to make the journey as stress-free as possible for your pet. This means protecting him from physical harm, as well as blocking out any stressful stimuli.

The best type of container to use when transporting your snake is a plastic storage box. Add several ventilation holes to the container to provide suitable ventilation and be sure that the lid fits securely.

Place a few paper towels or some clean newspaper in the bottom of the box in case your snake defecate or discharge urates. It is also wise to crumple a few of the layers of newspaper, which will provide a place in which your snake can hide.

Cover the outside of the transport cage if you are not using an opaque container, which will prevent your pet from seeing the chaos occurring outside his container. Check up on your snake regularly, but avoid constantly opening the container to take a peak. A quick peak once every half-hour or so is more than sufficient.

Pay special attention to the enclosure temperatures while traveling. Use your digital thermometer to monitor the air temperatures inside the transportation container. Try to keep the temperatures in the mid-70s Fahrenheit (23 to 25 degrees Celsius) so that your pet will remain comfortable. Use the air-conditioning or heater in your vehicle as needed to keep the transport cage within this range (because you cannot control the thermal environment, it is not wise to take your snake with you on public transportation).

Keep your snake's transportation container stable while traveling. Do not jostle the container unnecessarily and always use a gentle touch when moving it. Never leave the container unattended.

Hygiene

Reptiles can carry *Salmonella* spp., *Escherichia coli* and several other zoonotic pathogens. Accordingly, it is imperative that you use good hygiene practices when handling reptiles.

Always wash your hands with soap and warm water each time you touch your pet, his habitat or the tools you use to care for him. Antibacterial soaps are preferred, but standard hand soap will suffice.

In addition to keeping your hands clean, you must also take steps to ensure your environment does not become contaminated with pathogens. In general, this means keeping your snake and any of the tools and equipment you use to maintain his habitat separated from your belongings.

Establish a safe place for preparing his food, storing equipment and cleaning his habitat. Make sure these places are far from the places in which you prepare your food and personal effects. Never wash cages or tools in kitchens or bathrooms that are used by humans.

Always clean and sterilize any items that become contaminated by the germs from your snake or his habitat

Chapter 14: Common Health Concerns

Your water snake cannot tell you when he is sick; reptiles endure illness stoically. This does not mean that injuries and illnesses do not cause them distress, but without expressive facial features, they do not *look* like they are suffering.

In fact, reptiles typically do not display symptoms until the disease has already reached an advanced state. Accordingly, it is important to treat injuries and illnesses promptly – often with the help of a qualified veterinarian –in order to provide your pet with the best chance of recovery.

Finding a Suitable Veterinarian

Water snake keepers often find that it is more difficult to find a veterinarian to treat their snake than it is to find a vet to treat a cat or dog. Relatively few veterinarians treat reptiles, so it is important to find a reptile-oriented vet *before* you need one. There are a number of ways to do this:

-You can search veterinarian databases to find one that is local and treats reptiles.

-You can inquire with your dog or cat vet to see if he or she knows a qualified reptile-oriented veterinarian to whom he or she can refer you.

-You can contact a local reptile-enthusiast group or club. Most such organizations will be familiar with the local veterinarians.

-You can inquire with local nature preserves or zoos. Most will have relationships with veterinarians that treat reptiles and other exotic animals.

Those living in major metropolitan areas may find a vet reasonably close, but rural reptile keepers may have to travel considerable distances to find veterinary assistance.

If you do not have a reptile-oriented veterinarian within driving distance, you can try to find a conventional veterinarian who is willing to consult with a reptile-oriented veterinarian via the phone or internet.

These types of "two-for-one" visits may be expensive, as you will have to pay for both the actual visit and the consultation, but they may be your only option.

Reasons to Visit the Veterinarian

While snakes do not require vaccinations or similar routine treatments, they may require visits for other reasons. Anytime your snake exhibits signs of illness or suffers an injury, you must visit the veterinarian.

Visit your veterinarian when:

-You first acquire your snake. This will allow your veterinarian to familiarize himself or herself with your pet while it is presumably healthy. This gives him or her a baseline against which he or she can consider future deviations. Additionally, your veterinarian may be able to diagnose existing illnesses, before they cause serious problems.

-Your time your snake wheezes, exhibits labored breathing or produces a mucus discharge from its nostrils or mouth.

-Your snake produces soft or watery feces (soft feces are expected when snakes are fed some food items, such as birds. This is not necessarily cause for concern.). Intestinal prolapses also necessitate immediate veterinary care.

-Your snake suffers any significant injury. Common examples include thermal burns, friction damage to the rostral (nose) region or damaged scales.

-Reproductive issues occur, such as being unable to deliver young. If a snake appears nervous, agitated or otherwise stressed and unable to give birth, see your veterinarian immediately.

-Your snake fails to feed for an extended period. While many snakes fast from time to time – which is no cause for concern – a veterinarian should see any new snake that does not eat for 4 weeks. Snakes that have been in your care, and normally eat aggressively, may fast for longer than this without ill effects.

Ultimately, you must make all the decisions on behalf of your snake, so weigh the pros and cons of each veterinary trip carefully and make the best decision you can for your pet.

Just be sure that you always strive to act in his best interest.

Common Health Problems

While a wide variety of health problems can befall your snake, the majority will fall into one of the following categories.

Retained or Poor Sheds

From time to time, captive snakes fail to shed completely. This is particularly common among snakes that hail from high-humidity habitats, such as water snakes.

With proper husbandry, healthy snakes should produce one-piece sheds regularly (if the shed skin is broken in one or two places, but comes off easily, there is no cause for concern).

Retained sheds vary in their severity. Sometimes snakes simply fail to shed a small portion of scales, and other times, snakes may retain the majority of the old skin.

Retained sheds can cause health problems, particularly if they restrict blood flow. This is often a problem when a snake retains a bit of old skin near the tail tip.

If your snake sheds poorly, you must take steps to remove the old skin and review your husbandry to prevent the problem from happening again. If you are providing ideal husbandry parameters, and yet your snake still experiences poor sheds, consult your veterinarian to rule out illness.

The best way to remove retained sheds is by soaking your snake or placing him in a damp container for about an hour. After removing him, see if you can gently peel the skin off. Try to keep the skin in as few pieces as possible to make the job easier.

Do not force the skin off your snake if it will not come off easily; simply return him to his cage and repeat the process again in 12 to 24 hours. Usually, repeated soaks or time in a damp hide will loosen the skin sufficiently to flake off easily.

If repeated treatments do not yield results, consult your veterinarian. He may feel that the retained shed is not causing a problem, and advise you to leave it attached – it should come off with the snake's next shed. Alternatively, it if is causing a problem, the veterinarian can likely remove it.

Retained Spectacles
Spectacles are the clear scales that cover your snake's eyes. Sometimes, snakes fail to shed their spectacles, which can lead to serious medical problems in some cases.

Do not try to remove a retained spectacle yourself; simply keep the snake in a humid environment and take it to your veterinarian, who should be able to remove the retained scales relatively easily.

Respiratory Infections
Like humans, snakes can suffer from respiratory infections. Snakes with respiratory infections may exude fluid or mucus from their nose or mouth, be lethargic or refuse food. They may also spend excessive amounts of time basking on or under the heat source, in an effort to induce a "behavioral fever."

Bacteria, or, less frequently, fungi or parasites can cause respiratory infections. Additionally, cleaning products, perfumes, pet dander and other particulate matter can irritate a snake's respiratory tract.

Some infective bacteria and fungi are ubiquitous, and only become problematic when they overwhelm a snake's immune system. Other bacteria, as well as most viruses, are communicable, meaning that they are transmitted from one snake to another.

To reduce the chances of illnesses, keep your snake quarantined from other snakes, keep his enclosure exceptionally clean and be sure to provide the best husbandry possible, especially as it relates to temperature and humidity. You should also avoid stressing your snake by handling him too frequently or exposing him to chaotic situations.

Most respiratory infections require veterinary assistance. Your veterinarian will likely take samples of the mucus and have it analyzed to determine the causal agent. The veterinarian will then prescribe medications, such as antibiotics or antifungal medications, as appropriate.

It is imperative to carry out the actions prescribed by your veterinarian exactly as stated and keep your snake's stress level very low while he is healing, as stress can reduce immune function. You should also consider covering the front of his cage while he recovers.

Many snakes produce audible breathing sounds for a few days immediately preceding a shed cycle, which does not necessarily indicate a respiratory infection. This is rarely cause for concern and will resolve once the snake sheds. However, if you are in doubt, always seek veterinary attention.

"Mouth Rot"
Mouth rot – properly called stomatitis – is identified by noting discoloration, discharge or cheesy-looking material in the snake's mouth. Mouth rot can be a serious illness, and requires the attention of your veterinarian.

While mouth rot can follow an injury (such as happens when a snake strikes the side of a glass cage) it can also arise from systemic illness. Your veterinarian will cleanse your snake's mouth and potentially prescribe an antibiotic.

Your veterinarian may recommend withholding food until the problem is remedied. Always be sure that snakes that are recovering from mouth rot are kept in immaculately clean habitats with ideal temperature gradients.

Internal Parasites
In the wild, most snakes carry some internal parasites. While it may not be possible to keep a snake completely free of internal parasites, it is important to keep these levels in check.

Consider any wild-caught snake to be parasitized until proven otherwise. While most captive bred snakes should have relatively few internal parasites, they can suffer from such problems as well.

Preventing parasites from building to pathogenic levels requires strict hygiene. Many parasites build up to dangerous levels when the snakes are kept in cages that are continuously contaminated from feces.

Most internal parasites that are of importance for snakes are transmitted via the fecal-oral route. This means that eggs (or a similar life stage) of the parasites are released with the feces. If the snake inadvertently ingests these, the parasites can develop inside the snake's body and cause increased problems. Such eggs are usually microscopic and easily lifted into the air, where they may stick to cage walls or land in the water dish. Later, when the snake flicks its tongue or drinks from the water dish, it ingests the eggs.

Internal parasites may cause your snake to vomit, pass loose stools, fail to grow or refuse food entirely. Other parasites may produce no symptoms at all, which illustrates the importance of routine examinations.

Your veterinarian will usually examine your snake's feces if he suspects internal parasites. By looking at the type of eggs inside the snake's feces, you veterinarian can determine which medication will treat the problem.

Many parasites are easily treated with anti-parasitic medications, but often, these medications must be given several times to eradicate the pathogens completely.

Some parasites may be transmissible to people, so always take proper precautions, including regular hand washing and keeping snakes and their cages away from kitchens and other areas where foods are prepared.

Examples of common internal parasites include roundworms, tapeworms and amoebas.

External Parasites
The primary external parasites that afflict snakes are ticks and snake mites. Ticks are rare on captive bred animals, but wild caught snakes may be plagued by dozens of the small arachnids.

Ticks should be removed manually. Using tweezers grasp the tick as close as possible to the snake's skin and pull with steady, gentle pressure. Do not place anything over the tick first, such as petroleum jelly, or carry out any other "home remedies," such as burning the tick with a match. Such techniques may cause the tick to inject more saliva (which may contain diseases or bacteria) into the snake's body.

Drop the tick in a jar of isopropyl alcohol to ensure it is killed. It is a good idea to bring these to your veterinarian for analysis. Do not contact ticks with your bare hands, as many species can transmit disease to humans.

Mites are another matter entirely. While ticks are generally large enough to see easily, mites are about the size of a pepper flake. Whereas very bad tick infestations number in the dozens, mite infestations may include thousands of individual parasites.

Mites may afflict wild caught snakes, but, as they are not confined to a small cage, such infestations are somewhat self-limiting. However, in captivity, mite infestations can approach plague proportions.

After a female mite feeds on a snake, she drops off and finds a safe place (such as a tiny crack in a cage or among the substrate) to deposit her eggs. After the eggs hatch, they travel back to your snake (or to other snakes in your collection) where they feed and perpetuate the lifecycle.

Whereas a few mites may represent little more than an inconvenience to the snake, a significant infection can stress them considerably. In extreme cases, they may even lead to anemia and eventual death. This is particularly true for small or young animals. Additionally, mites may transmit disease from one snake to another.

There are a number of different methods for eradicating a mite infestation. In each case, there are two primary steps that must be taken: You must eradicate the snake's parasites, and eradicate the parasites in the snake's environment (which includes the room in which the cage resides).

It is relatively simple to remove mites from a snake. When mites get wet, they die. However, mites are protected by a thick, waxy exoskeleton that stimulates the formation of an air bubble.

This means that you cannot place your snake in water to drown the mites. The mites will simply hide under the snake's scales, protected by the air bubble.

To defeat this waxy cuticle, you can simply add a few drops of liquid soap to the water. The soap will lower the surface tension of water, allowing it to creep under the snake's scales. Additionally, the soap disrupts the surface tension of the water, preventing the air bubble from forming.

Soaking your snake is the slightly soapy water for about one hour will kill most of the mites on his body. Use care when doing so, but try to arrange the water level and container so that most of the snake's body is below the water.

While the snake is soaking, perform a thorough cage cleaning. Remove everything from the cage, including water dishes, substrates and cage props. Sterilize all impermeable cage items, and discard the substrate and all porous cage props. Vacuum the area around the cage and wipe down all of the nearby surfaces with a wet cloth.

It may be necessary to repeat this process several times to eradicate the mites completely. Accordingly, the very best strategy is to avoid contracting mites in the first place. This is why it is important to purchase your snake from a reliable breeder or retailer, and keep your snake quarantined from potential mite vectors.

As an example, even if you purchase your snake from a reliable source, provide excellent husbandry and clean the cage regularly, you can end up battling mites if your friend brings his snake – which has a few mites – to your house.

It may even be possible for mites to crawl onto your hands or clothes, hop off when you return home and make their way to your snake.

Make it a practice to inspect your snake and his cage regularly. Look in the crease under the snake's lower jaw, near the eyes and near the vent -- common places in which mites hide. It can also be helpful to wipe down your snake with a damp, white paper towel. After wiping down the snake, observe the towel to see if any mites are present.

Chemical treatments are also available to combat mites, but you must be very careful with such substances. Beginners should rely on their veterinarian to prescribe or suggest the appropriate products to use.

Avoid repurposing lice treatments or other chemicals, as is often encouraged by other hobbyists. Such non-intended use may be very dangerous, and it is often in violation of Federal laws.

New hobbyists should consult with their veterinarian if they suspect that their snake has mites. Mite eradication is often a challenging ordeal that your veterinarian can help make easier.

Long-Term Anorexia

While short-term fasts of a few weeks are common among snakes, those that last longer than this may be cause for concern. If your snake refuses food, ensure that its habitat is set up ideally with ample hiding opportunities and access to appropriate temperatures.

If none of these factors requires attention, consult your veterinarian. Above all, do not panic – snakes can go very long periods of time without eating.

Your veterinarian will want to make sure that your snake is in good health, as respiratory infections, mouth rot or internal parasites may cause him to refuse food.

Some snakes refuse food in the winter or breeding season, as they would in the wild. While you should consult with your veterinarian the first time this happens, it shouldn't cause you much concern in subsequent years.

A brown water snake.

Chapter 15: Breeding Water Snakes

Breeding water snakes is a relatively straightforward process, and requires only a few basic steps to complete. However, keepers must consider the prospect of captive reproduction carefully at the outset.

Pre-Breeding Considerations

Before you set out to breed your water snakes, consider the decision carefully. Unfortunately, few keepers realize the implications of breeding their snakes before they set out to do so.

Ask yourself if you will be able to:

- Provide the proper care for the female while gravid
- Afford emergency veterinary services if necessary
- Be willing to remove the young from the same cage hosting an angry, protective female.
- Provide housing for 20 or more babies
- Provide food for 20 or more babies
- Dedicate the time to establishing 20 or more babies
- Find the time to care for 20 or more babies
- Find new homes for 20 or more babies
- Afford to heat up to 20 baby snake habitats

Few people are able to do all of these things. But unfortunately, they see the price tags associated with many snakes, and instantly envision themselves becoming snake breeders. However, the vast majority of people that try to breed snakes for profit fail.

Becoming a snake breeder means that, depending on the area in which you live, you may have to obtain licenses, insurance or permits to do so legally.

Sexing Water Snakes

Obviously, you must have at least one sexual pair of animals to hope for reproductive success. In fact, it is wise to verify the sex of *all* snakes slated for breeding programs, except those who have successfully reproduced in the past.

However, determining the sex of water snakes (and most other snakes) is somewhat difficult, as their genitals are completely internal and they exhibit very few obvious signs that indicate their sex.

Experienced keepers often attempt a technique called manual eversion, in which gentle pressure is applied to the base of a snake's tail. If performed correctly, the pressure will cause the vent to open and the hemipenes (if present) to evert. Those with hemipenes are considered male and those that fail to evert hemipenes are considered female.

However, manual eversion is not an ideal method for determining a snake's sex. Males eventually become strong enough to resist the pressure, which would cause them to be mistaken for females. Accordingly, it is only a suitable technique for very young individuals – it is of little use with mature animals.

A technique called "probing" is generally considered to be the best method for determining the sex of your snakes. Probing involves the insertion of a smooth, blunt steel probe into a snake's cloaca.

The idea is that if the snake is a male, the probe will pass deeply into his tail, as it travels through one of the two inverted hemipenes. If the snake is a female, the probe will end at the base of a short, wide pocket, and only penetrate a short distance.

However, the person performing the technique must interpret the results to some degree, so misidentifications occur from time to time.

Because the technique requires a strong understanding of your snake's internal anatomy and some finesse, it is best for beginners to seek out knowledgeable keepers or veterinarians for assistance. Additionally, as improper techniques may lead to injuries, beginners should never attempt to probe an animal without proper instruction.

Pre-Breeding Conditioning
Breeding reptiles always entails risk, so it is wise to refrain from breeding any animals that are not in excellent health. Breeding is especially stressful for female water snakes, who must carry the developing young for several months.

Animals slated for breeding trials must have excellent body weight, but obesity is to be avoided, as it is associated with reproductive problems. Ensure that the snakes are appropriately hydrated, and are free of parasites, infections and injuries.

Cycling

Cycling is the terms used to describe the climactic changes keepers impose upon their animals, which seek to mimic the natural seasonal changes in an animal's natural habitat.

For example, keepers may simulate winter conditions by reducing the enclosure temperatures and providing fewer hours of lighting. These changes are often necessary to stimulate captive reptiles into producing eggs, sperm or both.

Successful breeders employ a wide variety of cycling regimens, but most involve a slight reduction in nighttime temperatures, and some also include a slight drop in daytime temperatures. Some keepers also allow the humidity levels to drop during the cycling period, or they manipulate the photoperiod to yield slightly longer nights and slightly shorter days.

For example, you may begin cycling your snakes in early November by allowing their habitat temperature to drop about 5 to 10 degrees Fahrenheit (about 2 to 6 degrees Celsius) and reduce the number daylight hours (and therefore the amount of hours that the basking spot is turned on) by one or two hours.

You would keep the temperatures in this range until the beginning of January, at which time you would restore the typical thermal environment, photoperiod and humidity levels. Some keepers actually increase the humidity immediately following cycling, to help simulate a rainy season.

However, because water snake species hail from different climates, it is important to consider the species and subspecies in question before establishing a cycling protocol. Those from the northern end of the group's range likely require cooler temperatures to stimulate successful reproduction than those from the southern end of the group's range do.

Some water snakes will begin refusing food with the onset of lower temperatures, while others will continue to feed.

Pairing

Once your water snakes have been cycled for 4 to 6 weeks, it is time to begin introducing the male to the female's enclosure.

Copulation may begin almost immediately, or it may take several hours to occur. The pair may copulate only once, or they may copulate several times over many days.

It is usually wise to house the pair together for several days, to allow for multiple copulations, thereby helping to ensure good fertility.

Always take the time to separate the animals before feeding attempts to prevent accidents. However, many water snakes (particularly males) will refuse food until after the breeding season reaches its conclusion.

Eliciting Copulation

Occasionally, males fail to court and breed the female with whom they are paired. Sometimes, there is nothing that can be done to change this – some pairs are simply not compatible. However, snake breeders have devised a number of techniques over the years that may help encourage copulation.

The presence of other males may incite the male's competitive instincts, and cause him to breed.

Some water snake breeders have noticed that copulation often occurs during thunderstorms. While you cannot control the weather, you can certainly take advantage of storms when they occur. If possible, open the windows to lower the barometric pressure in the room. Misting the snakes with water may also encourage breeding activity.

If you have tried every method possible to elicit breeding activity, and had no success, separate the animals and wait for one of them to shed. Place the animals back together immediately after the shed and hope for the best.

Ultimately, some pairs are just incompatible. In such cases there is little the keeper can do except try to switch animals and hope for better chemistry with a new pair.

Care of the Gravid Female

With some luck, the female will ovulate shortly after the animals have bred. When this occurs, the unfertilized ova are released from the ovaries and moved into the oviducts, where they are fertilized by waiting sperm.

While not always seen by keepers, ovulation causes a large swelling in the female's abdomen, particularly if both ovaries ovulate simultaneously. In extreme cases, the size of the bulge can exceed that produced by a large food item. This is typically not a cause for concern – to the contrary, ovulation ensures that the female will eventually deposit young or infertile eggs (often termed "slugs").

Ovulation typically lasts a matter of hours, but sometimes continues for 24 hours or more. After ovulation, the female can be considered gravid. Most females will shed their skin shortly after this occurs. This is referred to as the post-ovulation shed.

Remove the male from the female's enclosure once ovulation occurs or the female begins displaying such signs that she is gravid. This will help keep her calm and allow you to provide better care for her.

Do not handle gravid females unless absolutely necessary, and try to keep their stress level as low as possible. It is often wise to cover the female's enclosure to give her additional privacy.

Gravid females may alter their behavior in several subtle ways. They may bask for prolonged periods of time or become more reclusive. Some may adopt darker colors for the duration of the pregnancy. After initially exhibiting an increased appetite, most females cease feeding as parturition approaches.

Near the end of the gestation, females develop very plump abdomens. In some cases, they may lie on their sides or backs, in an effort to expose the developing embryos to overhead heat sources.

Parturition

Females may give birth to their entire litter relatively quickly, over the course of an hour or so, or it may take them several hours to complete the process.

Some of the young are likely to be born while still inside their transparent, membranous egg sacks, while others will have broken free while inside the mother's body.

After delivering all of the young, females may consume any slugs present. This behavior is thought to help the mother regain nutrients that would be lost otherwise, and it may also help to reduce odors that may attract predators.

Once you are sure the female has delivered the entire litter, it is wise to soak her for about 30 minutes. This will help wash off the byproducts of the labor process and give her a chance to rehydrate.

Be aware that some females become extremely defensive after giving birth. It may help to place a soft towel over her body, which will allow you to scoop up her body while keeping her relatively calm.

Remove the young while the female is soaking and perform a thorough cage cleaning to remove any lingering odor of parturition – some females may be reluctant to feed if they can still smell the litter.

Neonatal Husbandry

Begin by removing all of the young who have broken free of their egg sack and absorbed their entire egg yolk. You can place these individuals in a small, communal "nursery" until they complete their first shed.

A small plastic storage box makes a good nursery. You will need to heat the nursery with a heating pad or heat lamp, to keep it around 80 degrees Fahrenheit (26 to 27 degrees Celsius) at all times.

Keep the nursery simple, with a damp, paper-towel substrate and crumpled paper for hiding. You must also provide a wide, shallow water dish for the young snakes.

Young that have not yet emerged from their egg sacs or absorbed their yolks should be handled very delicately. Place each such snake in a separate enclosure, set up just like the communal nursery.

Do not attempt to break open the egg sack or pull on the egg yolk – simply be patient and keep such snakes warm and humid until they emerge on their own.

As they shed, individual snakes should be moved to their own enclosure. Begin feeding trials soon after their first shed. Many water snakes refuse food the first or second attempt, so patience is required. By contrast, others will feed readily at the first opportunity.

Chapter 16: Further Reading

Never stop learning more about your new pet's natural history, biology and captive care. This is the only way to ensure that you are providing your new pet with the highest quality of life possible.

It's always more fun to watch your snake than read about him, but by accumulating more knowledge, you'll be better able to provide him with a high quality of life.

Note: at the time of printing, all the websites below were working. As the internet changes rapidly, some sites might no longer be live when you read this book. That is, of course, out of our control.

Books

Bookstores and online book retailers offer a treasure trove of information that will advance your quest for knowledge. While books represent an additional cost involved in reptile care, you can consider it an investment in your pet's well-being. Your local library may also carry some books about water snakes, which you can borrow for no charge.

University libraries are a great place for finding old, obscure or academically oriented books about water snakes. You may not be allowed to borrow these books if you are not a student, but you can view and read them at the library.

Herpetology: An Introductory Biology of Amphibians and Reptiles
By Laurie J. Vitt, Janalee P. Caldwell
Top of Form
Bottom of Form
Academic Press, 2013

Understanding Reptile Parasites: A Basic Manual for Herpetoculturists & Veterinarians
By Roger Klingenberg D.V.M.
Advanced Vivarium Systems, 1997

Infectious Diseases and Pathology of Reptiles: Color Atlas and Text
Elliott Jacobson
CRC Press

Designer Reptiles and Amphibians
Richard D. Bartlett, Patricia Bartlett
Barron's Educational Series

Magazines
Because magazines are typically published monthly or bi-monthly, they occasionally offer more up-to-date information than books do. Magazine articles are obviously not as comprehensive as books typically are, but they still have considerable value.

Reptiles Magazine
www.reptilesmagazine.com/
Covering reptiles commonly kept in captivity.

Practical Reptile Keeping
http://www.practicalreptilekeeping.co.uk/
Practical Reptile Keeping is a popular publication aimed at beginning and advanced hobbies. Topics include the care and maintenance of popular reptiles as well as information on wild reptiles.

Websites
The internet has made it much easier to find information about reptiles than it has ever been.

However, you must use discretion when deciding which websites to trust. While knowledgeable breeders, keepers and academics operate some websites, many who maintain reptile-oriented websites lack the same dedication and scientific rigor.

Anyone with a computer and internet connection can launch a website and say virtually anything they want about water snakes. Accordingly, as with all other research, consider the source of the information before making any husbandry decisions.

The Reptile Report
www.thereptilereport.com/
The Reptile Report is a news-aggregating website that accumulates interesting stories and features about reptiles from around the world.

Kingsnake.com
www.kingsnake.com
After starting as a small website for gray-banded kingsnake enthusiasts, Kingsnake.com has become one of the largest reptile-oriented portals in the hobby. The site features classified advertisements, a breeder directory, message forums and other resources.

The Vivarium and Aquarium News
www.vivariumnews.com/
The online version of the former print publication, The Vivarium and Aquarium News provides in-depth coverage of different reptiles and amphibians in a captive and wild context.

Journals
Journals are the primary place professional scientists turn when they need to learn about water snakes. While they may not make light reading, hobbyists stand to learn a great deal from journals.

Herpetologica
www.hljournals.org/
Published by The Herpetologists' League, Herpetologica, and its companion publication, Herpetological Monographs cover all aspects of reptile and amphibian research.

Journal of Herpetology
www.ssarherps.org/
Produced by the Society for the Study of Reptiles and Amphibians, the Journal of Herpetology is a peer-reviewed publication covering a variety of reptile-related topics.

Copeia
www.asihcopeiaonline.org/

Copeia is published by the American Society of Ichthyologists and Herpetologists. A peer-reviewed journal, Copeia covers all aspects of the biology of reptiles, amphibians and fish.

Nature
www.nature.com/
Although Nature covers all aspects of the natural world, many issues contain information that reptile enthusiasts are sure to find interesting.

Supplies
You can obtain most of what you need to maintain water snakes through your local pet store, big-box retailer or hardware store, but online retailers offer another option.

Just be sure that you consider the shipping costs for any purchase, to ensure you aren't "saving" yourself a few dollars on the product, yet spending several more dollars to get the product delivered.

Big Apple Pet Supply
http://www.bigappleherp.com
Big Apple Pet Supply carries most common husbandry equipment, including heating devices, water dishes and substrates.

LLLReptile
http://www.lllreptile.com
LLL Reptile carries a wide variety of husbandry tools, heating devices, lighting products and more.

Doctors Foster and Smith
http://www.drsfostersmith.com
Foster and Smith is a veterinarian-owned retailer that supplies husbandry-related items to pet keepers.

Support Organizations
Sometimes, the best way to learn about water snakes is to reach out to other keepers and breeders. Check out these organizations, and search for others in your geographic area.

The National Reptile & Amphibian Advisory Council
http://www.nraac.org/
The National Reptile & Amphibian Advisory Council seeks to educate the hobbyists, legislators and the public about reptile and amphibian related issues.

American Veterinary Medical Association
www.avma.org
The AVMA is a good place for Americans to turn if you are having trouble finding a suitable reptile veterinarian.

The World Veterinary Association
http://www.worldvet.org/
The World Veterinary Association is a good resource for finding suitable reptile veterinarians worldwide.

References

Anderson, S. P. (2003). The Phylogenetic Definition of Reptilia. *Systematic Biology*.

BC, J. (1988). Muscular mechanisms of snake locomotion: an electromyographic study of lateral undulation of the Florida banded water snake (Nerodia fasciata) and the yellow rat snake (Elaphe obsoleta). *Journal of Morphology*.

F. BRISCHOUX, L. P. (2010). Insights into the adaptive significance of vertical pupil shape in snakes. *Journal of Evolutionary Biology*.

King, R. B. (1986). Population Ecology of the Lake Erie Water Snake, Nerodia sipedon insularum. *Copeia*.

Lígia Pizzatto, S. M.-S. (2007). Life-history adaptations to arboreality in snakes. . *Ecology*.

Index